SAUDI ARABIA

Hunt Janin

MARSHALL CAVENDISH
New York • London • Sydney

Reference edition published 1993 by
Marshall Cavendish Corporation
2415 Jerusalem Avenue
P.O.Box 587, North Bellmore
New York 11710

Editorial Director	Shirley Hew
Managing Editor	Shova Loh
Editors	Tan Kok Eng
	Leonard Lau
	Siow Peng Han
	MaryLee Knowlton
Picture Editor	Yee May Kaung
Production	Edmund Lam
Art Manager	Tuck Loong
Design	Ang Siew Lian
	Ong Su Ping
Illustrators	Lo Chuan Ming
	Kelvin Sim
Cover Picture	Obremski (The Image Bank)

Printed in Singapore

Originated and designed by
Times Books International
an imprint of Times Editions Pte Ltd
Times Center, 1 New Industrial Road
Singapore 1953
Telex: 37908 EDTIME Fax: 2854871

Library of Congress Cataloging-in-Publication Data
Janin, Hunt, 1940–
     Saudi Arabia / Hunt Janin.
          p. cm.—(Cultures of the world)
     Includes bibliographical references and index.
     Summary: Discusses the geography, history, government, economy,
and culture of the country that is Islam's birthplace and probably the
driest large country on the face of the earth.
     ISBN 1-85435-532-5 (vol.) :   —ISBN 1-85435-529-5 (set)
     1. Saudi Arabia—Juvenile literature.   [1. Saudi Arabia.]
I. Title.   II. Series.
DS204.J36 1992
953.8—dc20
                                                              92–13448
                                                                 CIP
                                                                 AC

INTRODUCTION

FROM THE DEPTHS of the Red Sea to the vast expanse of its sandy deserts and the gleaming spires of its many mosques, the Kingdom of Saudi Arabia is a spectacular country of great natural and man-made beauty. A look at the country's geography and geology reveals that Saudi Arabia is a desert kingdom, with a great deal of sun, little water and enormous amounts of oil locked in the sedimentary rocks of its eastern region. This harsh environment has produced a romantic but demanding Bedouin (nomadic) way of life, a world religion (Islam) and a modern kingdom still ruled by its founding family, the House of Saud.

Saudi Arabia's revenue from the sale of its oil has enabled it to make the desert bloom into modern cities, airports, hospitals, roads, ports and cropland. The Saudis themselves have adjusted remarkably well to the rapid but profound changes which in a short span of time have propelled them from a simple tribal society based on the camel into a prosperous nation based on oil. They now enjoy not only many of the advantages of a modern economy but, also the many benefits of their unique traditional culture.

As part of the series *Cultures of the World*, this book is an introduction to Saudi Arabia and its people, their lifestyle, language and social customs.

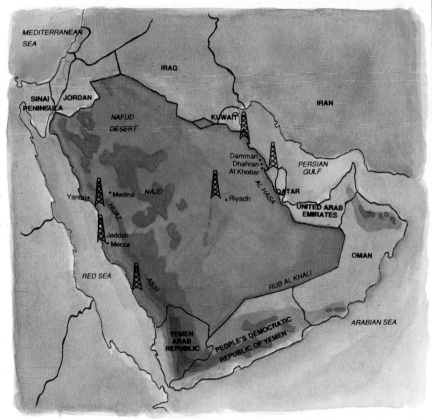

CONTENTS

A sculpture adorns a street in Jeddah.

4

CONTENTS

A Saudi and his camel, the "ship of the desert."

GEOGRAPHY

SAUDI ARABIA is a vast country. Occupying four-fifths of the Arabian Peninsula, it has an area of 865,000 square miles, nearly a quarter the size of the United States. It borders Jordan, Iraq and Kuwait to the north, Yemen and Oman to the south and the Persian Gulf, Qatar, and the United Arab Emirates to the east. It is separated from Egypt, The Sudan and Ethiopia by the Red Sea on the west.

Seen in its geographical entirety, Saudi Arabia is a huge, tilted plateau which rises sharply from the Red Sea in the west and then slopes gradually down to the Persian Gulf in the east. It is a land of extremes. The interior of the country contains many sharp mountain ridges and great areas of sand. Saudi Arabian mountains rise up more than 9,000 feet and can be freezing cold in winter. They tower above sand or gravel deserts where summer temperatures often exceed 120 F and where it rarely rains. There are no lakes, no permanent rivers, no big forests: Saudi Arabia is probably the driest large country on the face of the earth. It is not an easy or a soft land, but it does have an austere beauty all of its own.

Opposite: **Curving sand dunes are caused by winds blowing through Saudi Arabia's vast deserts. The greatest area of sand in the world is found here, in the vast Rub al-Khali Desert.**

Left: **Desert plateaus rise from a sea of sand in northwestern Saudi Arabia.**

The Red Sea borders Saudi Arabia on the west, separating it from the African continent.

GEOLOGICAL HISTORY

Big as the Arabian Peninsula is now, geologists think it is only a small piece of an even bigger land which existed a long time ago. The continents of Africa and the Arabian Peninsula were once fused together into a single mass. Later, however, due to heat and stresses deep within the earth, about 70 million years ago, this landmass began to split apart at the rift line now marked by the Red Sea.

The Arabian part of this mass—known as the Arabian plate—moved away, slowly but inexorably, to the northeast. During this long process (which is still going on), the Red Sea edge of the Peninsula rose up sharply, forming the western mountains of the Hijaz; the rest of the Arabian plate sloped down to the east toward the Persian Gulf. Subsequently, fiery lava fields covered much of the tilted Hijaz. But because the low eastern areas were under water, they received sedimentary deposits instead.

This explains why in Saudi Arabia oil is found chiefly in Al Hasa (the Eastern Province) or under the waters of the Gulf. Oil comes from the billions upon billions of tiny plants and animals which lived in the warm shallow seas that covered this area. When they died millions of years ago they rained down upon the bottom of the sea, and through the centuries formed sedimentary beds. In contrast, the upwellings of lava in the west did not contain similar plant and animal matter.

All the oil of the Gulf states—Iran, Iraq, Saudi Arabia, Kuwait, Bahrain, Qatar, and the United Arab Emirates—comes from the same geological formation known as the Arabian Platform. Together, these countries contain more than half of the world's proven oil reserves.

THE FOUR MAIN REGIONS

Saudi Arabia contains four main geographic regions—the Najd, Hijaz, Al Hasa and Asir.

NAJD With an average elevation of 2,000 to 3,000 feet above sea level, the Najd is a vast eroded plateau located in the central heartland of Saudi Arabia. Much of the Najd is desert: the Great Nafud in the north, the al-Dahna in the east and part of the immense Rub al-Khali ("roob ahl-KAH-li") in the south. The Najd is the traditional home of the ruling Saud ("Sah-OOD") family. Saudi Arabia's bustling capital, Riyadh ("Ree-AAD"), once a sleepy mud-walled village, is located here. The nomads who peopled the Najd are known for their generosity, bravery and love of poetry.

Eroded rocks in the Hijaz stay put and firm despite the ravages of time and human activities. The Hijaz has two zones, a narrow coastal plain and a mountain area. The latter contains wadis (valleys normally dry but carrying run-off water in the rainy season) which make sedentary habitation possible.

HIJAZ The Hijaz has the greatest variety of people, ranging from desert Arabs to the descendants of Africans. It is the most diverse region and lies in the west in the range of mountains that run parallel to the Red Sea coast. The Hijaz contains the narrow coastal strip known as the Tihamah, where the port of Jeddah is located. More importantly, the Hijaz contains the two holiest cities of Islam, Mecca and Medina.

AL HASA Al Hasa embraces the flat eastern coast of Saudi Arabia along the Persian Gulf. This region has lush oases, where farmers tend vividly green gardens in the midst of the desert. This is also where most of Saudi Arabia's oil is found and it is here that the great oil cities of Dhahran and Dammam are based, producing oil for the world. Much of Saudi Arabia's oil is shipped to world consumers by tankers loaded at Ras Tanura on the Gulf. Al Hasa has a population of 600,000, mostly Shiite Moslems.

ASIR The last geographical region is mountainous Asir, located in the southwest corner of Saudi Arabia near neighboring Yemen. Because its relatively generous rainfall makes terraced agriculture possible, the Asir was known to the ancient Romans as *Arabia Felix*—"happy" or "flourishing" Arabia. Its major city is Abha, perched at an elevation of about 8,000 feet.

The highlands of Asir has sustained a settled population from ancient times. Watered by the Indian Ocean monsoon, the Asir is the most fertile area in Saudi Arabia.

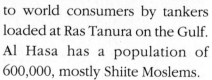

THE EMPTY QUARTER

Known as the "Empty Quarter," the Rub al-Khali, in the southeastern corner of Saudi Arabia, is the greatest continuous expanse of sand in the world. About the size of the state of Texas, it covers approximately 264,000 square miles—roughly one-third of the entire country. Virtually uninhabited and subjected to blistering heat in summer days and below-freezing temperatures in winter nights, the Empty Quarter is one of the driest and most desolate places on the face of the earth.

Some of the sand in this gigantic desert stays put, but much of it is blown about into curving dunes by the incessant, ever-shifting winds. A typical sand dune frequently assumes a U-shape, like a huge horseshoe. It can range in size from two to 500 feet in width and from 15 to 150 feet in height.

CLIMATE

Saudi Arabia's climate differs from one part of the country to another. The country has a dry climate, with high temperatures in summer in most areas with particularly high temperatures in the central and northern areas. In the south, however, the temperature is normally moderate, dropping on the Sarawat mountains in Asir to as low as 50 F in the summer. In winter temperatures generally become moderate, turning cold at night when it sometimes drops to below 32 F, especially on the western mountains and along the northern borders.

Because of climatic patterns, rain-bringing weather usually bypasses the Arabian Peninsula. Rainfall in most parts of Saudi Arabia is therefore uneven and unreliable. On the average, less than four inches of rain falls on Jeddah, Riyadh or Dhahran each year. But this figure masks big regional variations.

The real pattern is usually one of drought or cloudburst. Along the Red Sea coast, torrential rains can fall in March and April. The highlands of Asir can get more than 15 inches of monsoon rain per year. At the other extreme, however, a desert can go without any rain at all for 10 years at a time. But when rain does come to this parched land, the results are magical: seeds long hidden dormant in the earth suddenly bloom in a matter of hours and the apparently lifeless desert turns green for a few days.

Right: **The date palm has always played an important role in the life of the Saudi Arabians. While the wood of the tree is used for constructing houses, its fruit is used as food. As much as 600 pounds of fruit a year can be produced by a single date palm.**

Below: **Against the stark contrast of a desert, a single flower blooms, only to wither away as quickly as it blooms.**

FLORA

Except for parts of the rainy Asir, where wild olives and some larger trees grow, and in the scattered oases where date palms are cultivated, there are few true trees in Saudi Arabia. The types of plants that have adapted to the harsh environment are all hardy, drought-resistant and stunted. Most of them are brown or greenish-brown, except after infrequent rains, when patches of green herbs and colorful flowers can quickly bloom and wither. Often, hundreds of consecutive square miles of the country can be covered by drought-adapted species such as the *rimth* saltbush or the yellow-flowered *arfai*. In some parts, small tamarisk and acacia trees are common.

Saudi Arabia's flora may be limited, but it is quite unusual. The frankincense tree, for example, produces a dried resin which used to be exceedingly costly. Large amounts of frankincense were burned in the religious celebrations of the ancient Middle East to perfume ceremonies and sacrifices. One shrub, known as the "toothbrush bush," is used by the nomads to clean their teeth. Herbs of the desert are also used to season and preserve food, to make clothes sweet-smelling and for washing hair.

OASES

An oasis is a fertile place in the midst of a sand or gravel desert. Providing a green contrast with its dry surroundings it is a welcome sight to weary, thirsty travelers. Some oases consist merely of a few palm trees around a small spring or well. Others cover vast areas like the Al Hasa oasis which is supplied by water from more than 50 artesian springs. Covering a total area of 70 square miles, Al Hasa includes the towns of Hofuf, Mubarraz and many other villages and hamlets which support a vast permanent population. Tamarisk trees on the borders of the oasis help keep desert sand from spreading over the carefully tended gardens, which produce lush fruits, vegetables and grains, such as dates, citrus, melons, tomatoes, onions, rice, wheat, barley and henna (a reddish dye used by women to decorate their hands and feet and by men to tint their beards).

FAUNA

Wildlife inhabitants of Saudi Arabia include the wolf, jackal, hyena and baboon. Among the smaller animals are the fox, the hedgehog, the Arabian hare, the jerboa (kangeroo rat), and the ratel (honey badger). The gazelle, ibex, leopard and other larger mammals were once common throughout most of Arabia but their numbers are now much diminished, due to overhunting in the 1930s.

Since 1986, however, Saudi Arabia's National Commission for Wildlife Conservation has set aside eight reserves to protect threatened animals and plants. The first of these to be set up was a 5,237-square-mile reserve near Ta'if, which is not far from Jeddah. This reserve is a protected zone for endangered gazelles and the re-introduced oryx, which became extinct in the wild in the early 1960s.

Camels are magnificently adapted to life in the harsh desert and can go for long periods without drinking water. They have heavy eyelids and eye lashes to protect against the sun and sand.

Birds are a common sight in the Saudi kingdom. Large numbers of flamingos, storks, swallows and other birds cross the Arabian Peninsula during their annual migrations. Some winter in Saudi Arabia. Native birds include sand-grouse, larks, bustards, quail, eagles and buzzards. Gulls, pelicans and other water birds live along the coasts.

Many species of snakes, lizards and scorpions abound in the desert region. Domesticated animals include the camel, the chief support of nomadic life in the desert, horse, sheep, goat and donkey.

The coral reefs of the Red Sea provide food and shelter for the many fishes which live there, such as these butterflyfish.

THE CORAL GARDEN OF THE RED SEA

Besides its land creatures, Saudi Arabia's seas offer unparalleled panoramas of underwater life. The brilliantly-colored marine life of the long thin Red Sea (about 1150 miles long, 180 miles wide) is arguably the most spectacular part of Saudi Arabia's natural beauty.

The clear, warm shallow areas of this body of water provide the perfect environment for the growth of corals, which come in a wide range of sizes, shapes and colors. Their names suggest their rich diversity: there are hard, soft, black, fire (which can sting divers badly), brain (shaped like a giant human brain), mushroom, bushy and fan corals. Seen from underwater, these formations are so abundant and so beautiful that they are often referred to as "coral gardens."

To swim over the crest of a Red Sea reef while wearing a face mask and to look down at the bottom through 30 feet of clear, warm sunlit water is to see an unforgettable, colorful profusion of marine life. Among the harmless and most brightly colored fish in the coral gardens are parrotfish, butterflyfish, pennant fish, royal angelfish and coral trout. Some less common and more dangerous creatures include lionfish, stonefish, stingrays, moray eels and sharks.

CITIES OF THE KINGDOM

The major urban areas of Saudi Arabia are Riyadh, the capital, located in the interior; Jeddah, a key port and commercial center on the Red Sea; the Dhahran/Dammam/Al Khobar complex, the center of oil production, near the Gulf coast; and Mecca and Medina, the two holiest cities of Islam, in the western hills of the Hijaz.

An aerial view of Riyadh, the political and economic center of the nation. In less than 50 years, Riyadh has been transformed from a mud-walled town of 25,000 inhabitants to an international metropolis of 1.8 million people.

Riyadh When Abdul Aziz, the founder of the kingdom of Saudi Arabia, captured Riyadh in a camel raid in 1902, it was only a tiny mud-brick village lost in the wilderness of central Arabia. It remained something of a backwater until the sharp runup of oil prices after 1973 turned it into a boom town. The Saudis then wanted to modernize their capital and to do so quickly. They handled this rapid modernization process so well that Riyadh has grown more quickly than any other city in the Middle East.

Today, Riyadh is a sprawling modern city of about 1.8 million people, highlighted by modern buildings which combine the lines of traditional Arabic architecture with modern materials, air conditioning and other conveniences. Reflecting Riyadh's importance as a world capital, the entire diplomatic corps moved there from Jeddah in the 1980s. There are now roughly 90 embassies and other diplomatic missions in Riyadh, all located in a separate diplomatic enclave near the city.

Jeddah Traditionally known as the "Bride of the Red Sea," Jeddah is an ancient commercial port which handled much of the spice trade of the Red Sea and served as the gateway for pilgrims coming to nearby Mecca.

Modern Jeddah is characterized by the prevailing white color of its buildings. As a result of an extensive beautification scheme, the city has been transformed into an attractive tourist and commercial center.

Like Riyadh, Jeddah also grew explosively during the oil boom. The old harbor, which had become a bottleneck for the entry of badly-needed building materials and consumer items, was rebuilt into a modern port capable of handling 30 million tons of freight each year. A new airport covering over 40 square miles—the King Abdul Aziz International Airport —was constructed to ease the entry into the Saudi kingdom of the more than 1.5 million pilgrims who go on the hajj each year. The population of Jeddah is now about 1.6 million people. Many citizens think their city is more charming than Riyadh, even if it lacks the capital's political and financial importance.

Dhahran/Dammam/Al Khobar This port-city complex, consisting of Dhahran, Dammam and Al Khobar, has also experienced rapid growth in recent years. It is the home of the Arabian-American Oil Company (now owned by the Saudis and known as Saudi Aramco) and of the University of Petroleum and Minerals. The three oil cities, with a population of about

500,000, serve as an outlet to the world for the vast petroleum-gathering and petrochemical industries of Saudi Arabia's Eastern Province.

Mecca and Medina Mecca, formerly a market town for camel caravans, is the birthplace of Islam. Throughout its history, Mecca has been venerated as a holy place and attracted the Arab tribes from every part of the Arabian Peninsula. When the annual tide of the hajj pilgrims floods in, the population of Mecca temporarily approaches two million. Normally, however, the city is much smaller, with a population of about 850,000. Mecca contains the Grand Mosque with the great Ka'bah, the holiest shrine of Islam and the focal point of Islamic worship. After Mecca, Medina is the second most important city for all Moslems. It is the city where the Prophet Mohammed, the founder of Islam, took refuge to escape persecution. With a population of about 430,000, Medina's most venerated historical site is the tomb of Mohammed in the Prophet's Mosque. Medina also houses an Islamic University and the famous King Abdul Aziz Library, which contains 37,000 books on religious topics and a collection of rare copies of the Holy Koran, some in the form of manuscripts written hundreds of years ago.

The Medina Railway Station is a striking example of traditional Arabic architecture.

HISTORY

CIVILIZATION IN THE ARABIAN PENINSULA goes back many thousands of years. If there is any pattern evident over this long stretch of time, it is that periods of anarchy (when each region or nomadic tribe was a law unto itself) have alternated with periods of dynastic control (when there was a strong centralized government). The unsettled conditions during the decline of the ruling Ottoman empire, for example, were brought to an end by the founding of the modern kingdom of Saudi Arabia in 1932.

THE EARLIEST ARABS

In prehistoric times, Stone Age hunter-gatherers drifted out of eastern Africa into the Arabian Peninsula, which was then lush and well-watered. About 15,000 years ago, however, the weather grew warmer and the deserts began to spread. Some of the inhabitants became nomads herding camels, goats and sheep. Others settled in small villages around oases or along the sea coasts and supported themselves by agriculture and trade.

Wedged between three major continents, the Arabian Peninsula (Arabia) was an important passage for caravans of traders crisscrossing their way over the vast deserts, carrying frankincense and myrrh, silk and spices, gold, precious stones and ivory to Egypt, Palestine, Syria and ancient Babylon. Many of the early inhabitants of Arabia performed the important role of middlemen in this commercial link. One group, called the Nabateans, settled in the northwestern part of Arabia, where they built a stronghold at Madain Salih, to control this trade. In A.D.106, however, the Romans captured their capital at Petra to strengthen their own hold on the trade routes of the Peninsula. This military conquest marked the beginning of the end of the Nabatean civilization.

Opposite: **A building in a deserted town in ancient Dedan, in the northwestern part of Saudi Arabia. Situated along one of the major caravan routes, Dedan was an important city serving the ancient spice trade.**

Above: **The rock tombs and dwellings, built by the Nabateans at Madain Salih in northwestern Saudi Arabia, give us an idea of the Nabatean civilization which flourished on the rich spice trade some two thousand years ago.**

19

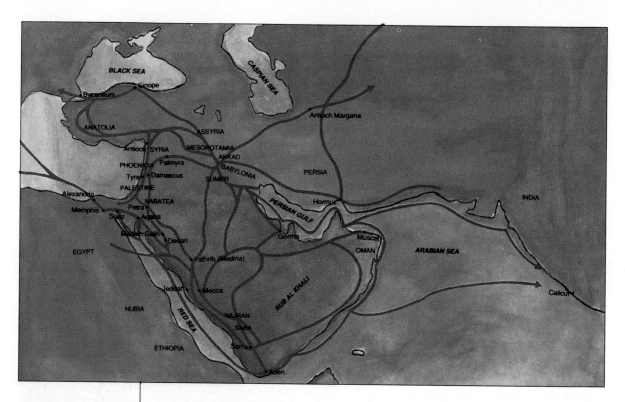

On the map, the following labels are visible:

BLACK SEA, Sinope, Byzantium, CASPIAN SEA, ANATOLIA, ASSYRIA, Antioch Margana, Antioch, SYRIA, MESOPOTAMIA, AKKAD, PHOENICIA, Palmyra, BABYLONIA, PERSIA, Tyre, Damascus, SUMER, PALESTINE, Alexandria, NABATEA, Hormuz, INDIA, Memphis, Petra, PERSIAN GULF, Suez, Aqaba, Gerrha, Muscat, Madain Salih, Dedan, Yathrib (Medina), OMAN, ARABIAN SEA, EGYPT, RUB AL KHALI, Jeddah, Mecca, Calicut, NUBIA, RED SEA, NAJRAN, SABA, ETHIOPIA, San'a, Aden

Above: **Saudi Arabia was an important trade cross-roads throughout most of its history.**

Below: **An old fort stands on a caravan route.**

Arabia continued to be a commercial crossroads but continued infighting among the Arab tribes for control of the trade routes caused the once prosperous trade to decline. By A.D. 200, parts of northern Saudi Arabia had been incorporated into the Roman province of Arabia. In the fourth and sixth centuries, south-western Arabia fell under Abyssinian rule. Throughout all these years the Peninsula remained politically fragmented. By the beginning of the sixth century, Arabia was still a collection of small warring states.

THE COMING OF THE PROPHET

The most important event, and a turning point in the history of the Arabian Peninsula, was the birth of the Prophet Mohammed, the founder of Islam, in A.D. 571. Within his life span Mohammed established a religion that was destined for a world role and laid the foundations of the Arab empire. Preaching the oneness of Allah, he became the temporal leader as Islam substituted a religious bond for the traditional tribal loyalties. A century later, the Arabs, carrying the message of God, rode out of Arabia and conquered a large part of the then civilized world .

MOHAMMED AND ISLAM

Mecca, where Mohammed was born, was a trading center for the camel caravans bringing goods along the Red Sea coast. Mohammed's parents died when he was young and he was raised by his grandfather, who was a guardian of the Ka'bah, a holy stone building which was a center of the Arabs' worship of jinn, or spirits.

Mohammed himself was poor but his prospects rose when, at the age of about 25, he married a rich widow fifteen years his senior. Although he was a good trader, Mohammed also had a strong religious inclination. After he was 40 years old, he would retreat to a cave outside Mecca to pray and meditate on ways to improve the morality of his society. Tradition says it was there that the archangel Gabriel revealed to him the word of God.

Mohammed's first convert was his wife Khadija. By about 613 he was publicly preaching about what had been revealed to him. His followers wrote down what he said and in so doing gradually compiled a holy book, the Koran, which they believed had been dictated to Mohammed by God. Other Meccans, however, strenuously objected to his teachings because they threatened to stop the jinn worship at the Ka'bah and thus hurt Mecca financially. To escape persecution, in 622, Mohammed and some of his followers moved to a neighboring city, first known as Yathrib and later as Medina. This migration now marks the starting point of the Moslem calendar.

Mohammed's great talents gradually propelled him into a commanding military and political position in Medina. In 630, his forces conquered Mecca, where he transformed the Ka'bah into a shrine for Moslems and treated the vanquished Meccans with dignity and honor. Most of them soon became followers of Islam. When Mohammed died in 632, he had founded what was shortly to become a new world religion.

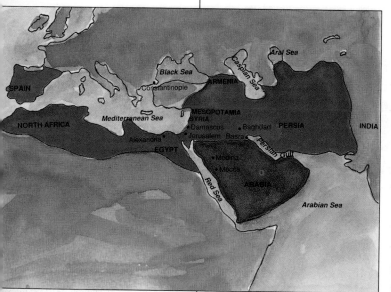

The expansion of Islam from A.D. 622 to 750. Following the death of Mohammed in A.D. 632, Islam expanded as a religious and political force and by the middle of the 8th century had established itself in Egypt, North Africa and Spain to the west and Syria, Persia, Afghanistan and parts of India to the north and east.

THE EXPANSION OF ISLAM

By the time of Mohammed's death in A.D. 632, the unification of the Arabian Peninsula was making good headway. Later, under the Umayyad dynasty (661 to 750) which ruled from Damascus, Islam spread rapidly, eventually reaching west into Spain and North Africa, north into Syria and Mesopotamia, and east into Aghanistan and parts of India.

But financial problems and feuding among the Arab tribes weakened this dynasty and it was eventually overthrown. In its place arose the Abbasid dynasty (750 to 1258), which from its capital in Baghdad presided over the "golden age" of the Arab/Islamic empire. Reaching a peak of glory under the rule of Caliph Harun al-Rashid and his son, the great mosques and palaces of Baghdad made it a world center of wealth and military power.

But a gradual economic decline set in, sealing the fate of the Abbasids. In 1258, the Mongols sacked Baghdad: the last caliph was kicked to death and the streets of the city were piled high with corpses.

MAMLUK AND OTTOMAN RULE

The Mamluks were a military caste that ruled Egypt from 1250 to 1517. During the 14th and 15th centuries they also controlled the Hijaz, including Mecca, Medina and Jeddah. In 1517, however, the Ottoman (Turkish) sultan, Selim I, conquered Egypt and assumed control of the Hijaz. His successor, Suleiman the Magnificent, spent huge amounts of money on fabulous new buildings for the holy cities of Islam.

THE GREAT ALLIANCE

In time, the Ottoman empire became weakened. Two important figures arose in the Najd, the heartland of the nomads. The first was an 18th century Moslem preacher, Mohammed ibn Abdul Wahhab, who wanted to purify Islam and rid it of the Persian and mystical influences which in his view had tainted it badly. The second was a local sheikh ("SHAY-k") of the Najd region, Mohammed ibn Saud, who wanted to protect and expand the territory his tribe controlled. The ambitions of these two men dovetailed nicely and in about 1750 they decided to join forces.

SETBACKS AND TRIUMPH

The sons of Mohammed ibn Saud and Abdul Wahhab continued the ambitious plan of expansion which their fathers had begun. By 1804, they had taken control of the holy cities of Mecca and Medina and had established a political/religious state embracing almost one million square miles of the Arabian Peninsula.

Their very success, however, aroused the hostility of the Ottoman Turks, who sent forces to punish them. The Turks recaptured the holy cities and, in about 1818, the ancestral home of the Saud family in the Najd as well. Thus the House of Saud's first effort to found a kingdom ended in failure.

A second effort began about 1820 but it, too, failed—this time because a rival family, the Rashid dynasty, eventually seized Riyadh from Saud control in 1891 and forced the Saud family to flee to neighboring Kuwait. There the family waited for the opportunity to regain its lost lands.

This chance finally came when Abdul Aziz ibn Saud (also known as Ibn Saud, "son of Saud") led 40 companions into the desert and in a daring camel-back raid captured Riyadh in 1902 after fierce hand-to-hand fighting.

The foundations of modern Saudi Arabia was laid by King Abdul Aziz Ibn Saud. Under his rule, Arabia was transformed from one with divided tribal allegiances into a unified nation.

THE FATHER OF SAUDI ARABIA

Abdul Aziz ibn Saud was a very tall, physically powerful, highly intelligent leader. He was a devout Moslem and spent part of each day in prayers and religious reading. To win the allegiance of the scattered, independent tribes of the desert, he briefly married and then divorced (strictly in keeping with the customs of Islam—by not having more than four wives at a time) a very large number of women.

Abdul Aziz himself claimed that he had married more than 282 wives and had fathered over 46 sons and many daughters. By the time of his death it is clear that he had fathered at least 58 officially-recorded sons and an unrecorded number of daughters. These offspring form the core of the huge royal family of today.

Below: **T.E. Lawrence's headquarters at Azraq Castle in Jordan during World War I.**

Opposite top: **T.E. Lawrence, better known as Lawrence of Arabia.**

Opposite bottom: **Relics from the blown Hijaz railroad still survive in the Arabian desert to this day.**

THE UNIFICATION OF SAUDI ARABIA

After capturing Riyadh, Abdul Aziz spent the next decade fighting the Rashid dynasty who had the support of the Ottomans, but without much success. He finally hit on the idea of uniting the nomads and encouraging them to settle down. This he did by creating a religious brotherhood, which he called the *Ikhwan* ("brethren"), to spread the puritanical Wahhabi gospel favored by the nomads.

In 1914, backed by *Ikhwan* fighters, Abdul Aziz captured most of central Arabia and the Eastern Province and pushed the Turks from the Gulf coastline. At this time, however, the western region, the Hijaz, was under the rule of another rival, Hussein. Enlisting the help of the famous British adventurer and soldier, Lawrence of Arabia, Hussein defeated the Ottoman Turks at Aqaba and proclaimed himself King of the Hijaz. The conflict between Hussein and Abdul Aziz for supremacy was inevitable. In 1925, after years of fighting, Abdul Aziz conquered the Hijaz region, including Mecca. In 1932, he unified Al Hasa, the Najd and the Hijaz into a new country known as the kingdom of Saudi Arabia.

LAWRENCE OF ARABIA

During World War I, the Arabs launched a revolt in Mecca to expel the Ottoman Turks and their German allies from the Middle East. But the Turks rallied quickly and sent men and supplies from Syria down the Hijaz railroad to Medina. The British had promised to help the Arabs attack the Turks. A young British archeologist who became an intelligence officer, Captain Thomas Edward Lawrence, volunteered to teach the Arabs how to wage a guerrilla war against the Turks.

In his famous and beautifully written account of this campaign, entitled *Seven Pillars of Wisdom,* Lawrence described how, by speaking Arabic well, becoming an excellent camel rider and by wearing resplendent white Arab robes, he was able to lead the Bedouin forces to victory. In 1917, together with about 30 camel-mounted nomads, he set out through the searing heat of the Hijaz mountains in northwestern Saudi Arabia to capture the strategic port of Aqaba, at the northern tip of the Red Sea.

Expecting to be attacked only from the sea because of the supposedly impassable desert behind them, the Turks in Aqaba had all their artillery pointed out to sea, toward the Gulf of Aqaba. Their guns could not be swiveled around and brought to bear on the land approaches to the city. In a brilliant surprise attack by land, after a grueling trip through the desert, Lawrence and the Arabs succeeded in capturing Aqaba.

In addition, by blowing up the Hijaz railroad, Lawrence and his forces also bottled up the Turkish army in Medina and forced other Turkish soldiers into a hopeless effort to defend the trains. The dramatic successes of this small-scale guerrilla warfare contributed to the eventual Allied victory in the Middle East.

Top: **An influential figure in the Arab world, King Faisal was noted for his outspoken views on Israel and the Soviet Union. Domestically, he was active in economic and educational reforms.**

Bottom: **A modest man and peacemaker, King Khalid was a popular ruler. When he died in June 1982, he was mourned throughout the kingdom.**

THE DEVELOPMENT OF A MODERN STATE

Saudi Arabia's stability owes much to the fact that a single dynasty has governed since Abdul Aziz ibn Saud established the kingdom in 1932. This was further enhanced by the discovery of oil in 1938, and the oil wealth it created, which made it possible for King Abdul Aziz to begin the transformation of the country into a modern state.

Saud, the eldest son of Abdul Aziz, became king when his father died in 1953. In 1964, King Saud abdicated in favor of his brother, Faisal ("FY-suhl"), who ruled successfully until his assassination in 1975. Faisal's rule saw the implementation of a program which started Saudi Arabia's drive towards modernization. Faisal was succeeded as king by his half-brother, Khalid. Economic development continued rapidly, thanks to the rapid rise of oil prices. More significantly, King Khalid's reign saw the setting in motion of the Second Development Plan which brought about further improvements in the people's economic and social standards of living.

When King Khalid died in 1982, his brother Fahd ("FAAH-haad") became the fourth and present king. King Fahd continues to lead the country along the road of development and progress although he has had the difficult task of managing the adjustment of the Saudi economy to the sharp fall in oil prices in the 1980s. He was the country's first Minister of Education and adopted an educational strategy that still serves as a guideline for the country's present educational system.

FOREIGN POLICY

Saudi Arabia has traditionally been on very good terms with Western countries, especially the United States, but has had few relations with communist states. The Saudi kingdom itself usually plays a cautious, low-key role in the diplomacy of the Middle East. One of its major concerns has been finding a solution to the Arab-Israeli conflict and the Palestinian problem.

Saudi Arabia has two main foreign policy objectives: to defend itself against any hostile foreign power, and to cooperate with other oil-producing countries as well as the major oil consumers.

THE GULF WAR

Iraq's unprovoked attack on its neighbor, Kuwait, in August 1990 posed a real dilemma for Saudi Arabia. Both the Saudis and the Americans feared that Iraq would try to capture the rich oil fields in the eastern part of the Saudi kingdom.

King Fahd with President Bush, 1989—a bond of friendship and trust.

The Saudis recognized they did not have the military power needed to stop an invasion by Iraq. But they were also concerned that inviting large numbers of foreign troops into their country would tilt the Kingdom too visibly toward the West. In the end, however, King Fahd decided that the wisest course of action was to join forces with the Americans and their allies in hopes of defeating Iraq as quickly as possible.

Thus, five days after the Iraqi attack on Kuwait, U.S. troops began to arrive in Saudi Arabia. In November 1990, the United Nations Security Council authorized the use of "all necessary means" to expel Iraq from Kuwait. When Iraq failed to withdraw, the Gulf War began in January 1991.

During this short, sharp conflict, in which the ground fighting itself lasted only 100 hours, more than 600,000 troops from 37 countries were deployed to Saudi Arabia. The war cost the Saudi government an estimated $37.5 billion. Without Saudi Arabia's full military and financial cooperation, the United States and its allies could not have won the war so quickly.

GOVERNMENT

SAUDI ARABIA is a monarchy with the Koran as the constitution. The king heads the government as the prime minister and also as president of the Council of Ministers.

The present king of Saudi Arabia is, to give him his preferred title and full name, King Fahd bin Abdul Aziz Al Saud, "The Custodian of the Two Holy Mosques." He is the eighth son of the founder of the modern state of Saudi Arabia, King Abdul Aziz, and the fourth king of the royal House of Saud.

The king combines in his person all the major functions of government — executive, legislative and judicial. In the tradition of the desert, however, sheikhs could never wield absolute power. They were chosen by the tribe as the best men for the job and they had to rule in accordance with public opinion. An informal but well-understood set of checks and balances helps to keep the Saudi kings in their proper role, which is to lead the country and to keep in close, friendly contact with their own people.

Saudi Arabia is not governed by a written constitution but by a body of Islamic law known as the *Sharia*. The body of law is, in turn, based on the holy book of Islam, the Koran. The *Sharia* makes it clear what the duty of a political and religious leader is: he must always rule for the common good. If he does not, he can be deposed. This is one important restraint on the king's power. Another check on an absolute monarchy is the concept of equality, which has its roots in the fierce independence of Bedouin life. All men are equal when they face the rigors of the desert. Islam also teaches that since all men are equal before God, they should bow to God alone, not to other men. As a token of this fundamental equality, at formal meetings Saudis may address the king with considerable familiarity: simply as "Ya Fahd!"— the equivalent of "Oh Fahd!" This informality reflects the fact that King Fahd rules with the consent of his people and not by the old European notion of the "divine right of kings."

Above: **Widely known for his interest in education, King Fahd has adopted an enlightened approach to transform Saudi Arabia into a modern state. Under his rule, he has established Saudi Arabia as a steadying influence in world affairs.**

Opposite: **The Palace of Justice in Riyadh where the processes of law are carried out.**

29

Located in the diplomatic quarters of Riyadh, the Ministry of Foreign Affairs building is also situated close to the offices of the King and the Council of Ministers' Complex. All the major policy-making decisions are made in Riyadh.

NATIONAL AND LOCAL GOVERNMENT

The king appoints a Council of Ministers, which has numerous legislative, executive and administrative duties and a considerable say in what goes on at the national and local level. The king, however, can veto the Council's decisions and can replace its ministers at will.

Just recently, the ruling family announced major political reforms with the setting up of a more representative "Consultative Council" consisting of 60 appointed members to share authority with the government and advise the Council of Ministers. The members are expected to be chosen from the academia, business and friendly religious elite. Besides reviewing laws and government policies, the Consultative Council is empowered to recommend that the king reject those laws or policies that are found lacking. But the king remains the final arbiter of state affairs.

The setting up of the Consultative Council, in effect, meant the broadening of the participation of Saudi citizens in their own government. With its implementation, the ancient structure of Saudi society based exclusively on tribal and paternalistic systems of government will change as the Saudi

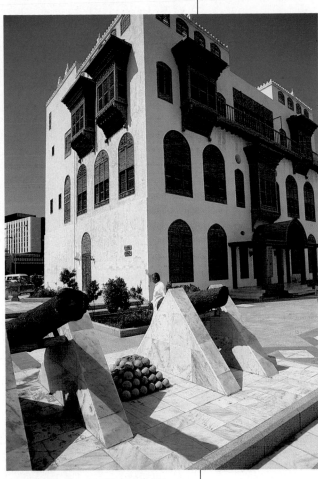

The British Legation in Riyadh. The moving of the entire diplomatic corps from Jeddah to Riyadh in the mid-80s is an indication of the growing importance of Riyadh as a world city.

royal princes no longer have a monopoly on decision-making.

For administrative purposes, Saudi Arabia is divided into six large provinces and twelve smaller administrative units. The names of the provinces reflect the geographic areas they cover: Western, Central, Southern, Southwestern, Eastern and Northern. An emir, a governor appointed by the Ministry of the Interior in Riyadh, is in charge of each province. He is an important person because he is usually a member of the royal family and oversees general administration in the province (including finance, health, education, agriculture and the cities) and helps to maintain law and order.

Despite this apparent decentralization, however, in practice Saudi Arabia is run very much from the top down—that is to say, all the important decisions are made in Riyadh. There are no self-sufficient elected local governments, as there are in the United States, at the city and state level. In the Kingdom, all the local administrative units depend entirely on Riyadh for policy guidance and for money. Riyadh, in turn, assumes full responsibility for their support. Apart from the election of some low-level advisors to help the chief municipal executives, there are no elections in Saudi Arabia.

HOW DECISIONS ARE MADE

Decisions at all levels in Saudi Arabia, whether national, local, tribal or family, are made only after an informal, usually lengthy process of discussion and consultation. One goal is to make sure that all views are heard, not only so that good ideas will come to the surface but also to give everybody a chance to participate personally and have a say in the decision-making process.

Personal participation is most noticeable in the daily *majlis* ("public audience") held by high officials. Each day, for example, Prince Sultan, the governor of Riyadh, reads petitions presented to him in person by a long line of supplicants. He then passes the petitions on to an aide for appropriate action.

The real purpose of this time-consuming process is not to make decisions quickly or efficiently. Instead, it is to build a consensus (a general agreement) such that Saudi citizens will respect and obey decisions which may affect their own lives. Indeed, one of the king's most important responsibilities is to find enough common ground between different elements of the society so that a consensus can eventually be reached.

KEEPING THE PEACE

Given the frequent wars in the Middle East, Saudi Arabia is lucky: it has been blessed by relative peace and stability ever since it was formally created in 1932. It has never been invaded by another country, although it seems Iraq planned to do so at the beginning of the Gulf War in 1991. There has been one attempted insurrection, in 1979, when a wild-eyed, heavily-bearded religious fanatic and his followers seized the Grand Mosque in Mecca and held out for a week before being captured and executed. But there have been no other challenges to the House of Saud.

Saudi Arabia's special relationship with the United States, coupled with its own armed forces, has helped to keep the peace. In addition, the Saudis have also spent billions of their oil dollars on defense, investing in a highly sophisticated air defense network and buying a great deal of other advanced weaponry from the West. Moreover, to reduce the need to call in foreign troops, after the Gulf War the Saudis reportedly decided to triple the total size of their own ground forces to around 200,000 men.

The Kingdom's armed forces must also be able to defend the House of Saud itself in case of an internal uprising. This is where the National Guard comes into play. Historical if not literal descendants of the Wahhabi Bedouin warriors (the *Ikhwan*) who fought for King Abdul Aziz and were later suppressed by him, the enlisted men of the National Guard are still simple tribesmen whose primary duty is to protect the royal family against any internal opponents.

A well-trained body, the Saudi National Guard plays a vital role in maintaining the country's internal stability.

33

ECONOMY

ORIGINALLY BASED on subsistence agriculture and funds brought in by pilgrimages, the economic structure of Saudi Arabia was completely transformed by the rapid rise of oil prices in the 1970s. The Kingdom's revenue from the sale of its oil has allowed Saudi Arabia to design and finance ambitious development projects which have set world records in terms of size and cost.

The full extent of Saudi Arabia's petroleum resources is still not known: oil companies keep finding more oil and gas than they can produce. But it is clear that Saudi Arabia has roughly 25% of the world's proven reserves of crude oil while its gas reserves are the fifth largest in the world.

More than 95 % of all Saudi oil is produced on behalf of the Saudi government by the Saudi Arabian Oil Company (Saudi Aramco). The Japanese-owned Arabian Oil Company and the U.S.-based Getty Oil Company (now owned by Texaco) provide the rest of Saudi crude oil production. Affiliates of the Saudi government's General Petroleum and Minerals Organization (Petromin) handle oil refining and blending, as well as the production and marketing of refined petroleum products.

Because Saudi Arabia has so few other resources and is the world's leading oil exporter, the petroleum sector is still the mainspring of the economy, contributing two-thirds of government revenues and 90 % of the country's export earnings.

Above: **Located to the north of Dhahran on the Gulf, Ras Tanura is the world's largest petroleum port.**

Opposite: **A worker on an oil rig. Oil rigs are located mainly off the Gulf coast where most of the oil is found.**

Saudi Arabia's production of crude oil and the value of that oil vary considerably from year to year depending on the economic forces of supply and demand. Oil prices can be quite volatile. During the 1980s, for example, the price of oil in the world market ranged from a high of about $40 per barrel to a low of about $10 per barrel. In 1991, Saudi Arabia was producing an unusual amount of oil to make up for the oil which could not be shipped from Kuwait and Iraq due to the 1991 Gulf War. Oil was traded at about $17 per barrel, relatively low compared to the highs reached during the oil boom.

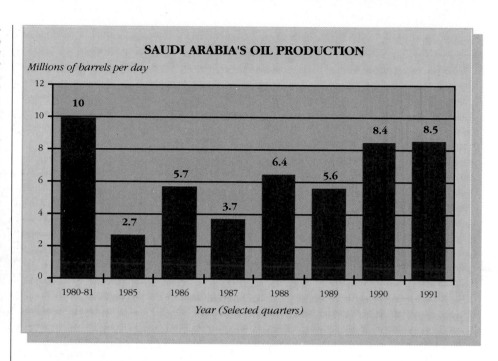

SAUDI ARABIA'S OIL PRODUCTION

Millions of barrels per day

Year (Selected quarters)

THE UPS AND DOWNS OF THE OIL MARKET

Saudi Arabia produces and sells oil chiefly in response to the ever-changing forces of supply and demand in the world oil market. Sometimes, there is too much oil on the world market and prices tumble. This may be good news for consumers (it means that gasoline and other forms of oil-based energy will be cheap) but it spells trouble for the producers of oil because their income falls and plans to develop their countries must be shelved.

Historically, the oil industry has waged a long, usually unsuccessful effort to keep the price of oil steady and high. OPEC (the Organization of Petroleum Exporting Countries) was founded in 1960 by Saudi Arabia and other major oil exporters for precisely this purpose. But the cycle of boom-and-bust still continues. The high prices of the 1970s were followed by the oil glut and low prices of the 1980s. By mid-1991, this surplus of oil had produced predictable results. Gasoline in the United States was selling at historic lows after inflation had been taken into account, and the economy of Saudi Arabia remained in an extended recession.

BLACK GOLD: THE MANY USES OF PETROLEUM

Petroleum (crude oil) is a thick, dark liquid which will burn and produce energy under the right conditions. It consists of mixtures of complicated chemical compounds known as hydrocarbons. At a refinery, crude oil is changed into other products which are essential for the smooth functioning of modern societies.

Nearly half of all the petroleum refined becomes gasoline, which powers everything from cars to lawn mowers and small airplanes. Another product is diesel fuel, used for trucks, ships and trains. Fuel oils are also important, as distillate for heating homes, and as residual for heating big buildings and powering ships and industrial plants.

But these are not all the uses of "black gold." Refining also produces petrochemicals—chemical compounds coming from the hydrocarbons of petroleum. Both natural gas and refinery by-products are used to make petrochemicals, which in turn are transformed into a wonderful variety of end products: plastics, artificial rubber, man-made fibers for clothing, fertilizers for farms, additives for food, high explosives, dyes, cosmetics, paint, ink, solvents, resins and drugs.

FINDING AND PUMPING OIL

A geologic "trap" is one of the requirements for an oil or gas field because it prevents the oil and gas from rising to the surface of the earth and escaping. Looking for traps is therefore an important first step in finding oil.

In Saudi Arabia, geologists often use sound waves, generated by small explosions, to look for traps. The sound waves bounce off rocks hidden deep in the ground. Some of these impulses are reflected back to the surface and are recorded on a sensitive instrument known as a seismograph. Although a seismograph cannot show whether there is any oil in a particular formation, it does give an accurate picture of its geological structure. Geologists can then estimate the probability of oil being found there.

Using a rotary drilling rig, oil men in the Kingdom drill wells deep into promising rock formations. Wells can also be drilled offshore in the Gulf, either from special ships or by three-legged "jackups" which rest on the bottom of the sea. Because there is so much oil under eastern Saudi Arabia and the Gulf, finding more is easier than it would be in other parts of the world. No matter where the oil is found, the next step is to get it out of the ground.

Oil in the earth is under natural pressure. If the pressure is high enough, it will flow up the well to the surface without any assistance. When the pressure is very high, it can produce a dramatic gusher, which must be capped and brought under control so the oil and gas forced up into the air will not go to waste. The Saudis are especially lucky: not only do they have the world's biggest oil field (the Ghawar field, 150 miles long and about 10 miles wide), but their oil is also under enough natural pressure so that it flows very readily, without the need for much pumping. This makes it easy and cheap to produce.

PIPELINES AND SHIPS

Once Saudi Arabian oil has been brought to the surface, it must be moved to world markets. This is done by pipelines and ships.

Local pipelines in eastern Saudi Arabia gather crude oil and gas from the Ghawar and other fields and deliver it to the petroleum-handling port of Ras Tanura on the Gulf, where tankers take it out of the Gulf to ports with refineries. Some oil is refined in the Kingdom itself but it has usually been more economical for the Saudis to ship crude.

A geologist uses a seismograph to help in the exploration of oil in the desert.

The most important pipeline from a strategic point of view is the Petroline system, which carries oil and gas from the eastern fields of Saudi Arabia all the way across the country to the petrochemicals facility and port of Yanbu on the Red Sea, 750 miles to the west. This route has the great advantage of avoiding a vulnerable bottleneck, especially in the narrow Strait of Hormuz at the mouth of the Gulf, which might be mined or otherwise

closed in the event of war, thus preventing the export of Saudi petroleum. Yanbu offers not only security but also efficiency: large amounts of oil can be stored there safely, tankers can be loaded quickly and a state-of-the-art computerized control room oversees the port's complex operations.

In the past, because of the high cost of transportation, refineries had to be built near oil fields, not near the urban areas which actually paid for and used gasoline and other fuels. Big tankers, however, lowered shipping costs appreciably. Thus, much Middle Eastern crude goes to the deepwater ports in Europe, of which Rotterdam in the Netherlands is the largest and best-known, and is refined there, close to the ultimate consumers. Saudi Arabia has plans to expand its own facilities to refine more oil and manufacture petrochemicals.

Oil is loaded by pipe-lines on to tankers at Ras Tanura. The refinery at Ras Tanura processes more than 500,000 barrels of crude oil daily.

The Hajj Terminal at the King Abdul Aziz International Airport in Jeddah is one of many infrastructural facilities built by the Saudi government. Another sector of growth is telecommunications. Saudi Arabia has the second most developed telecommunications system in Asia after Japan.

DEVELOPING THE DESERT

The oil boom of the 1970s gave Saudis the money and the opportunity to build an ultra-modern economy in the desert, with entirely new cities, airports, ports, hospitals, schools, roads and communication facilities.

The new industrial city of Jubail gives an idea of the speed and scale of the modernization process. Located on the Gulf coast of Saudi Arabia, Jubail is the biggest public works project in the modern history of the world. Construction began in 1976 and eventually engaged more than 50,000 workers from about 60 different countries. Huge amounts of earth were moved by bulldozers and dredges, enough to build a wall 23 feet wide and more than three feet high around the earth at its widest point. Jubail's cooling system, which brings seawater by canal from the Gulf to cool industrial machinery, is the largest in the world.

The King Khalid International Airport at Riyadh was opened in 1983. It has the world's tallest control tower (243 feet) and covers an area of 86 square miles. The beautiful Hajj Terminal at the King Abdul Aziz Airport in Jeddah, opened in 1981, was inspired by the sweeping lines of Bedouin tents. With the biggest roofed structure in the world, covering 370 acres, it is the main entry point for the hajj pilgrims who go to Mecca each year

Congestion at the port of Jeddah once forced ships to wait for weeks to unload. This led to delays in construction projects because supplies and equipment were bottled up in the port. But Jeddah, too, was modernized and now has 50 of Saudi Arabia's best piers. Yanbu, also on the Red Sea, has been developed as the Kingdom's second port, both to take some of the burden off Jeddah and to handle oil and petrochemical exports.

MAKING THE DESERT BLOOM

Saudi Arabia realizes that, vast as it is, its reserves of oil and gas are only finite. As they eventually dwindle or as alternative sources of energy become cheaper, the Kingdom will have to fall back on a more diversified economy if it is to maintain a high standard of living. At the same time, Saudis themselves must be trained to do much of the work now done by foreigners. For these reasons, Saudi Arabia has been investing heavily in other sectors of the economy, for example, in agriculture, aviation, manufacturing, mining and fishing, and is teaching Saudi citizens how to work in these fields.

This diversification can be quite dramatic. Seen from the air, the big green circular wheat fields near Riyadh are an unexpected sight. These are the result of modern pivot-centered irrigation systems which are more than half a mile in diameter and which successfully produce high-quality wheat. Thanks to the high prices offered by the government of Saudi Arabia, farmers in the country can now grow more than double the amount of wheat their country needs. The excess is exported to other Gulf states.

Saudi Arabia also exports a variety of fruit, such as figs and grapes. With sufficient water and the country's ceaseless sunlight, much of its light wind-blown soil can literally be made to bear fruit.

Above: **An efficient irrigation system has transformed Al Kharj from a barren landscape of sandy, parched soil to verdant wheat fields.**

Below: **A sprinkler-type irrigation system.**

Provision shops such as this friendly neighborhood store keep longer hours to cater to their neighborhood clientele.

A TYPICAL WORKDAY

A typical workday for a modern middle class Saudi family is in some respects similar to that of an American family in the 1950s: the father leaves the house and goes off to work at an office, the mother stays home to run the household, the children go to school.

The pace of office work in Saudi Arabia is usually more relaxed than it is in the United States. Less attention is paid to being physically present in the office during all the hours when it is officially open. Saudi government offices are, in theory, open from 7:30 a.m. until 2:30 p.m., but not all officials will be there for that full period of time. Private businesses operate from 8:00 a.m. until noon and then again from 3:00 p.m. to 6:00 p.m. Markets and shops stay open until 9:00 p.m. The owners or their relatives are likely to be at their shops during most of this time.

All trading ceases during prayer times, which occur five times a day between sunrise and sunset. The first prayers are offered after dawn but before sunrise. The next prayers are roughly at noon. An afternoon prayer and two final prayers (at sunset and in the late evening) round out the religious day.

Although Saudi Arabia has an excellent telephone network, much government and private business is still done on a traditional, face-to-face basis. Whenever possible, Saudis prefer to have personal ties with high officials because of the great importance of close interpersonal relations in Saudi culture.

FOREIGN WORKERS

Much of the work in Saudi Arabia is done by foreigners. By 1985, nearly half of the work force in the country consisted of Western and non-Western expatriates: for example, Yemenis, Filipinos, Sri Lankans, Koreans, Egyptians, Pakistanis, Palestinians and Westerners. The oil glut and recession since then have seen the departure of many of these foreigners, but virtually all of the heavy manual labor and much of the technical and professional work in Saudi Arabia is still done by non-Saudis.

There are several reasons for this. The basic one is that, thanks to oil, the Saudis can afford hired help. But population and cultural patterns are also involved.

For one thing, there are not many Saudis and the scale of the work that has to be done is enormous. King Khalid International Airport alone needs about 10,000 employees, ranging from janitors to computer experts and pilots. In addition, since Saudi women are strongly encouraged to be homemakers and mothers rather than taking jobs outside the home, and since they can work only in positions where they do not come into contact with men, relatively few Saudi women are in the labor force. The work they might otherwise do is therefore done by foreigners.

Moreover, many medical, technical and professional jobs are highly specialized and require a level of training and education which relatively few Saudis now have. Until young Saudis can be trained to fill these demanding jobs, a process which is being pushed hard by the government, there is no alternative to employing foreigners for the work.

Foreign workers account for a large percentage of Saudi Arabia's labor force. Some work in the technical and professional fields, while others are involved in construction work.

SAUDI ARABIANS

MANY SAUDI ARABIANS TODAY are direct descendants of the ancient nomads whose name comes down to us through the ages as "Aribi" or "Arabu" and who are now known as Arabs. These early Arabs lived in the northern deserts of the Arabian Peninsula and invented the camel-herding way of life still followed by some of the Bedouins in the Kingdom.

But because the isolation of desert life kept these ancestral Arabs from mingling very much with other peoples, many Saudis are considered to be "pure" Arabs. One sign of this is that they are ethnically homogeneous—in other words, they look very much alike—and, presumably, much like their nomad ancestors. It is this consciousness of their pure desert background and their pride in being the guardians of the holy cities of Mecca and Medina which give modern Saudis the self-confidence and generosity for which they are internationally known.

Opposite and below: **Saudi Arabians are generally descended from the nomadic tribes that inhabited the Arabian Peninsula. There are few racial minorities in Arabia and the population is essentially a homogeneous one.**

Some racial mixing did however occur along the fringes of the Arabian Peninsula. On the Red Sea coast, for example, some of the foreign pilgrims who came to Mecca from many parts of the world for the hajj stayed there and were absorbed into the native population. Africans also migrated to this region. Thus, in Jeddah today, there are Saudis with African backgrounds. Similarly, far to the east, migrants from Iran and India also settled down on the Gulf coast and intermarried with the local people. Some Saudis in the Al Hasa region today reflect this Persian and South Asian influence.

Nevertheless, unlike the United States and some other countries, Saudi Arabia has never been a real melting pot of different cultures and different peoples. Today, the only ethnic minorities are the 3 to 4 million foreigners working in the Kingdom, usually on short-term contracts. Technically, they are therefore neither an ethnic nor a religious minority.

A FEW PEOPLE IN A BIG LAND

For both political and cultural reasons, the size of Saudi Arabia's population is not known with much precision. Moreover, Saudi Arabia does not have a tradition of data-gathering. In a nomadic society, facts and figures simply did not have the importance they assumed in more urban cultures. There has not been a published census since 1974 and estimates of population size vary widely. One reasonable guess is that there are about 7.5 million Saudis in the Kingdom. Whatever the exact number, it is clear that in a huge land, roughly the size of the United States east of the Mississippi River, there are not many people. The population is also relatively young, with a median age of under 20 years. And with the population's high growth rate (somewhere between two and three percent each year), the number of children will continue to increase rapidly.

Dressed in the traditional *thobe,* a shopkeeper sells the ubiquitous *gutra,* the headcloth for Saudi men.

NATIONAL DRESS: THOBE AND VEIL

The blistering sun of the desert and the conservative traditions of the nomads have combined to produce a striking combination of national dress—one style for men, another for women.

Saudi men generally wear a long white robe, *thobe* ("thOb"), made of cotton for hot weather and light wool for cooler times. On the head is a skull cap, over which they drape a flowing head covering or *gutra*. In summer, a light white *gutra* of cotton is preferred because it is cool. In winter, a warmer red-and-white checked version is worn. A heavy doubled cord (*agal*), often black and traditionally used to tie up camels, holds the *gutra* in place.

Men often carry "worry beads" and finger them when negotiating business transactions. These beads (usually 33 on a circular string) probably originate from Islamic prayer beads. They can be made from a wide variety of materials such as plastic, silver, wood, ivory or semiprecious stones and are run through the fingers of one or both hands to ease tension in stressful situations.

47

In the past, a Bedouin man never felt well-dressed unless he was also well-armed. He usually carried a dagger, knife, sword and spear.

Later on, rifles—together with leather bandoliers worn across the chest to hold cartridges for the rifles—replaced the spears. Today, weapons are worn only for special ceremonial occasions.

The most distinctive feature of traditional Saudi dress for women is the veil. Practiced in the Middle East since at least 1500 B.C., face veiling has a practical purpose: it protects a woman's face from the desert sun and windblown sand. It also complies with the very strict requirement of conservative Islam that a woman take every possible precaution to safeguard her modesty. Nevertheless, veils can also be alluring. They are traditionally arranged so that only a woman's eyes, beautifully enhanced by kohl, a black cosmetic, are visible.

In the last decade, many Saudi women in Jeddah, probably the most open and least conservative city in Saudi Arabia, have been going out of their homes unveiled. Even these comparatively liberated ladies, however, still take pains to make sure they keep their heads, hair and bodies well-covered.

This they manage with another striking and traditional feature of women's dress—the *abaaya,* a long, black outer cloak which drapes a woman from head to ankle (except for part of her face, which is usually covered by a veil) when she leaves the privacy of a home. It, too, has a practical use: it is warm in winter and prevents the evaporation of the body's moisture in the summer. Like

The plain black cloak, *abaaya,* is preferred by today's Saudi women. Worn draped from the center crown, it is a very practical garment.

48

the veil, the *abaaya* also protects a woman's modesty, by keeping almost all of her body out of sight.

In the last few years some modern Saudi dress designers have copied, with good effect, the long flowing lines of traditional women's clothing in the Kingdom and have created colorful, graceful modern dresses which are a lovely blend of old and new.

HONOR AND THE NEED TO SAVE FACE

One of the best bits of folklore from the Saudi past is the story of a Bedouin sheikh who was known as the "Benefactor of the Wolves." Whenever he heard a wolf howling near his tent, he would order a servant to take a goat out into the desert, tether it there and then return to the camp. The reason—the sheikh insisted on being a good host. "No guest," he is reported to have said, "shall call on me in the evening without dining." It would not be honorable, he felt, to let any guest —not even a hungry wolf—leave his camp without being properly fed.

After Saudi Arabia was established, garments with motifs featuring the Kingdom's emblem of a palm tree surmounting two crossed swords became popular. These came in lengths of royal purple, parrot green, peacock blue, buttercup yellow and fire-engine red.

By greatly exaggerating the Saudi commitment to hospitality, this story also points out the great importance of honor in Saudi culture. A desert warrior once remarked, "Bedouin can be roused to do anything for honor." The flip side of the coin of honor, however, is the need to save face, in other words, to preserve one's honor at all costs. Thus, even at the risk of bankrupting himself by his open-handed hospitality to all visitors, the sheikh felt he had to maintain his reputation as a generous host. Had he failed to do so, he would have been ashamed, and in Saudi Arabia shame is the mortal enemy of a man's self-confidence and self-respect.

THE END OF AN ERA

Oil riches have meant the gradual passing of nomadic life. The glamor and romance of this roaming existence probably always seemed more attractive to foreigners and to urban Saudis than to the Bedouins themselves. Nomadic life originally developed out of sheer necessity—it was the only way people could survive in the desert. But it is a such a hard way of life that few people would follow it voluntarily.

Perhaps only 5% of the Bedouins are still full-time nomads. Most of them are now only semi-nomadic or have settled down permanently, a process actively encouraged by the government of Saudi Arabia through financial and other forms of help. Thanks to the government's policy of letting the oil wealth trickle down through the whole society, for the first time a new generation of Bedouins has other alternatives. Young nomads no longer literally have to follow in their fathers' camel-steps. Some will choose to do so, but most will acquire the job skills of the modern world—driving trucks, serving in the National Guard or working in the oil industry. As a result, their own descendants may learn about traditional Bedouin life only through tales told by their grandparents.

SOCIAL CLASS

Mohammed proclaimed that all people are "equal children of Adam." He asserted that God does not pay attention to tribal rank or race but only the sincerity of a Moslem's beliefs and the works of charity one performs during one's lifetime. This belief in the fundamental equality of all is a cornerstone of Moslem social thought. Perhaps as a result, compared with many other societies in the world, there are surprisingly few overt signs of class distinction in Saudi Arabia today.

Nevertheless, social classes do exist. At the very top of the social pyramid is, as might be expected, the House of Saud itself, consisting of the many descendants of King Abdul Aziz. Next in line are the old merchant families, often from Jeddah, who have vast fortunes (derived from trade) which predate the oil boom. They have money, but little political power.

Opposite: **A Bedouin and his worldly possessions.**

Above: **Modern Saudis are trained to cope with an increasingly technological world.**

Below them is a growing middle class, composed of technocrats, small businessmen and mid-ranking civil service officials. This group is becoming more important as national policies of "Saudization" (replacing foreign technicians with Saudi technicians) and diversification (developing sources of national income other than petroleum) begin to take hold. They are the Saudis with the most hands-on experience in actually running a modern state.

Because manual labor is considered "ignoble," Saudis usually refuse to do it; there is thus no Saudi blue-collar working class in the cities. In rural areas, however, there are the small farmers and in the deserts, the remaining nomads. These two interest groups may be at the bottom of the barrel socially, but politically they are still very important as the royal family needs their support to stay in power.

A SAUDI TALENT: ADJUSTING TO RAPID CHANGE

Since the oil boom of the 1970s, Saudi Arabia has undergone rapid social change. From a background of relative poverty, the country has become immensely rich, at times with an income of about $300 million a day. An educated middle class has developed. More children go to school. Medical care has improved. In short, within twenty years, between the early 1970s and the early 1990s, the Kingdom has changed enormously.

Shifts this dramatic and far-reaching can often be unsettling. In Saudi Arabia they have not been. In fact, what is striking is how effortlessly the Saudis seem to have adjusted. The Bedouins, for example, now move their camels around in Japanese pickup trucks. They also have water tankers to supplement the shallow wells of the desert. They used to be out of touch; now, thanks to transistor radios, they can hear about developments on the other side of the world within hours of their occurrence. A country which used to have few means of transportation now has its own national airline, Saudia. Saudi pilots fly some of the world's most advanced planes and span oceans and continents with ease.

The Saudis have been able to adjust so well to all these changes because several other important anchors in their lives have not changed. The House of Saud has remained in power so there has been continuity at the very top. The most important social unit, the family, has remained intact and has probably been strengthened by the country's general prosperity. The Kingdom's conservative interpretation of Islam is still the basis on which society runs smoothly. The perennial tug-of-war between Saudi moderates and Wahhabi conservatives over the proper pace of social change has been kept within familiar bounds. And, finally, high school and college students, so often an explosive force in other societies, have not challenged the status quo.

Opposite: Training for the future—students at the University of Petroleum and Minerals, Dhahran. Since its founding in 1963, the University has established a solid reputation as a leader in its field. Today, it has an international student body of about 4,000 and a teaching staff from all parts of the world.

LIFESTYLE

MODERN SAUDIS take great pride in their Bedouin past and in the rapid economic development of their country which has occurred under the leadership of the royal family. They are strongly committed to the welfare of all members of their extended families. Their religion, Islam, is also very important to them. All these national characteristics have deep roots in Saudi culture.

THE FAMILY: FIRST, LAST, ALWAYS

Since at least Biblical times, the family has been the only safe haven in the hostile environment of the Arabian Peninsula. It was not until the creation of the kingdom of Saudi Arabia in 1932 that there was any central authority which could keep the peace and punish transgressors. Under these conditions, the family became supremely important. Individuals simply could not survive on their own.

Traditionally, "family" meant the extended family. Covering at least three generations, the extended family usually included the father and mother, their unmarried children, and their married sons who had wives and children of their own. Other relatives were often included, too. For example, a divorced woman could not live alone but would return to the house of her father or another male relative. By the same token, a widow would move in with her son or son-in-law.

In Saudi Arabia today, this pattern in changing. Married children prefer to set up their own households if they can afford it. The classic three-generation extended family, all living under the same roof or in the same compound, is no longer the rule, especially in the cities. The new, smaller, nuclear family has inherited at least four of the key traits of the old extended family.

Opposite: **A Saudi father enjoys a cup of coffee and the companionship of his son.**

Taking a trip together—a farmer and son in Al Hasa.

The first of these is the central importance of the male leader of the family. Descent is patrilineal—children are identified only through their father as ibn or bin Khalid, "son of Khalid," or bint Khalid, "daughter of Khalid"—and the oldest male is the unquestioned head of the family, the patriarch. When family decisions are made, he is the one who finally decides what should be done after hearing the views of other members of the family. The mother has a great behind-the-scenes influence on her children, but she is not the formal decision-maker.

A second trait is that the survival and prosperity of the group (the family) itself is considered to be much more important than the wishes of any individual in it. Because of his seniority, the patriarch is thought to be the one most able to identify the best interests of the group. Other family members are expected to go along with his decisions no matter what their personal feelings may be. The individualism found in the United States and some other Western cultures therefore has no place in the Saudi way of life, particularly if it is expressed by women.

A third holdover from the days of the extended family is that most social activities take place only within the family group. Saudi families usually do not go out to restaurants or to public events such as fairs and festivals. Non-official entertaining is done in family homes, which offer the great advantage of privacy. On the other hand, keeping up with all the achievements and setbacks of parents, brothers, sisters, children and other relatives is almost a full-time job. It requires a constant exchange of visits and does not leave much time for other social activities outside the family circle.

A last inheritance from the extended family is the most important—personal security. The family is still the real safety net of Saudi society. It is a matter of family pride and honor that members take good care of each other. A person may be old, sick, unemployed, divorced, widowed, handicapped—whatever the problem, the family will provide emotional support and money.

In the past and on a bigger scale, the tribes of the Arabian Peninsula used to play much the same social role as the extended family does today. Tribal leaders gave their followers moral and financial support when they were alive and tried to avenge them when they were killed in battle with other tribes. Over the past thirty years, however, city life and the rapid economic development of the country have made tribal ties less relevant to many Saudis.

All that is best in the Arabs has come to them from the desert: their deep religious instinct, which has found expression in Islam; their sense of fellowship, which binds them as members of one faith; their pride of race; their generosity and sense of hospitality; their dignity and the regard which they have for the dignity of others as fellow human beings; their humor, their courage and patience, the language which they speak and their passionate love of poetry.

—Wilfred Thesiger,
in Arabian Sands

THE ROYAL FAMILY

The most dramatic example of the Saudi family as a mutual aid and protection society is the royal family itself. Like other families, the House of Saud takes pains to make sure its foundations are firm.

At the very apex of the power pyramid formed by the House of Saud is King Fahd. Crown Prince Abdullah (King Fahd's half-brother), who is next in line to become king, is second in terms of rank. Slightly further down the pyramid, three of King Fahd's brothers are in key positions. Power has been shared with a new generation, too. King Fahd's son Mohammed is the governor of the oil-rich Eastern Province. The late King Faisal's son, Saud, is the Foreign Minister of Saudi Arabia. And Prince Sultan's son Bandar (nephew of King Fahd) is Saudi Arabia's ambassador to the United States.

These arrangements at the most senior levels ensure that political and military power will remain with the royal family.

Thanks to its preeminent political position, the House of Saud is in a much better position than lesser families to make sure its financial position is secure. The staggering wealth of the royal family, however, must be spread around. Because King Abdul Aziz had so many children, the royal family is huge. It is actually a mini-tribe numbering about 6,000 people. As in other families, all these people have a claim, great or small, to a share of the House of Saud's riches. The more successful members of this royal tribe must see to it that their poorer relatives are not penniless.

Royal lifestyles vary a great deal. Some princes have huge palaces and lead an extravagant jet-set life. Others live modestly and devote themselves to business or good works. Much like the members of other Saudi families, the members of the royal family understand very clearly that their own well-being is directly related to the well-being of the House of Saud as a whole. They therefore carefully cultivate and nurture family relationships, consulting other family members and getting their approval before taking any major decisions. As in other Saudi families, the interests of the family as a whole, and not the wishes of any particular family member, are what makes this social system work.

A GROWING MIDDLE CLASS

Not all Saudis are princes or nomads. Many Saudi men and women are now well-educated and form a prosperous but not super-rich middle class. Often trained in the United States, they know the culture of the West but prefer to live and work in their own country. Their lifestyle is much closer to the Western than to the traditional Arabian Peninsula model. This new middle class may be the bridge between the petroleum-based Saudi Arabia of today and the more diversified, technically-proficient Saudi Arabia of the future.

The Saudi middle class live in houses with only a limited number of rooms or in apartments. They usually own these houses or apartments, borrowing the money to pay for them from Saudi banks, which give generous loans for just this purpose. The men hold down government jobs or else go into private business. In most cases, the woman's place is in the home, caring for the children. Girls in school are encouraged to study science as well as language and the arts.

Even though this group of people may study or work in the West for considerable periods of time, they continue, perhaps more in their hearts than in their outward behavior, to adhere to the religious teachings and customs of their own country. They know that their travels abroad are for specific purposes. Once their goals have been achieved, almost all of them will return to the Kingdom. This basic faithfulness to their own traditions makes it easy for them to readjust to the restrictions of Saudi culture when they get back home.

Apartment living is a feature of modern Saudi life. As the cities get increasingly packed, high-rise buildings are constructed to accommodate the urban population growth.

MEASURING TIME

Saudis have inherited from their nomadic past a very relaxed attitude toward most commitments based on time, for example, business appointments, hotel reservations, airline schedules, sports events and social engagements.

In Saudi eyes, time is too often the master of Western culture. They themselves are much more comfortable with time as their servant. Thus the "correct" time for a 10:00 a.m. meeting is not when the clock itself says 10:00 a.m., but when they themselves are able to get to the place where the meeting will be held.

This relaxed view about time is neatly summed up in the very common Arabic phrase, *Insha Allah* ("God willing"), as in "I will meet you at the hotel at 10:00 a.m., *Insha Allah.*"

Time in Saudi Arabia is measured by the Islamic calendar. It takes as its starting point the Hijrah (July 16, 622), when Mohammed moved from Mecca to Medina. From this beginning, time is subsequently reckoned according to the lunar calendar which has 354 days. Years are designated AH, meaning Anno Hegirae (in Latin, "the year of the Hijrah"). By using comparative tables, AH dates can be translated into CE (Christian Era or Common Era) dates. For example, the year 1413 AH corresponds to 1992 CE.

The weekend is also different in Saudi Arabia. Because Friday is a day of rest and prayer, the weekend falls on Thursday and Friday, not on Saturday and Sunday. This fact is frequently forgotten by businessmen and officials in other countries, who sometimes try, unsuccessfully, to telephone their Saudi counterparts during the Saudi weekend.

MIGRATION AND HOUSING

One consequence of the oil boom of the 1970s was a great migration of Saudis from the countryside to the cities. They were drawn there by the prospects of high-paying jobs, good schools and hospitals, and better opportunities for their children to learn business and administrative skills. This flow of people is still continuing today.

To help these migrants, the Saudi government provides subsidized housing, usually on the outskirts of the big cities, for low income groups. All building plots are first enclosed by a high wall so that the family will have privacy. A modest one or two-story house is then built in one corner of the property. The rest of the land is given over to sheep, goats and motor vehicles.

THE BEST HOSPITALS IN THE MIDDLE EAST

The royal family wants the oil riches to be shared with the general population. It therefore provides free medical care, not only for Saudi citizens but also for foreign Moslems who come to the Kingdom for the hajj (pilgrimage). When intractable medical problems cannot not be treated in-country, Saudi patients, plus one or more family members to keep them company, are sent at government expense to hospitals abroad.

The building of the $300 million King Faisal Hospital and Medical Center in Riyadh is a striking example of the enormously improved system of health care now available in Saudi Arabia. Its state-of-the-art facilities provide specialized treatment for patients who in the past would have to be sent abroad. More than 1,200 staff are engaged in keeping medical standards high. In addition, there are more than 210 other hospitals, with about 35,000 beds, in Saudi Arabia. The King Khalid Eye Specialist Hospital, also located in Riyadh, is one of the best. It has done good work treating trachoma, an eye disease which can lead to blindness. Doctors, nurses and technicians serving in these hospitals come from many countries of the world. As more Saudis are trained in medical skills, they will supplement and eventually replace these foreign specialists.

Opened in 1975, the King Faisal Hospital and Medical Center in Riyadh offers different specialized fields of treatment from heart disease to eye ailments and disorders of the nervous system. The hospital is also equipped with the latest diagnostic machines and one of the largest closed-circuit television systems in the world.

61

Saudi boys lead a less restrictive life than their female counterparts. As they grow older, more of their time is spent in the company of their fathers while the girls are progressively confined to the home and to the company of females.

THE CYCLE OF SAUDI LIFE

In nomadic life, parents valued boys more than girls. A boy would grow into a warrior who could defend his own tribe. When he married, his wife and children would become part of and would strengthen the parents' extended family. A girl, on the other hand, could not fight. After puberty, her sexual honor could be compromised, bringing shame to the family. When she married, she would weaken the extended family by leaving it to join her husband's. The birth of a boy was therefore a cause for great celebration. The birth of a girl aroused much less enthusiasm.

This traditional preference for boys continues today. When a woman bears a son, she assumes a new name: *umm* ("mother of"), followed by the name of her son. Until she has a son, she is only *bint* ("daughter of"), followed by the name of her father. Little boys get special treatment. They are breastfed longer than girls and become the favorites of the *hareem* (better known in English as "harem," this Arabic word only means "women's quarters"). At the same time, little girls are learning the subdued behavior which is appropriate for women.

As they grow up, however, boys come in for a rude shock. By the age of seven, they leave their pampered childhood behind and become part of their father's world—a more disciplined world of men, where they must do as they are told. Girls remain in the world of women, where they prepare for their future roles as wives and mothers.

EDUCATION: AT HOME AND ABROAD

Traditional education in Saudi Arabia involved memorizing and reciting large blocks of the Koran. Saudi educational policy today is still firmly grounded in the study of Islamic beliefs. It also tries to convince students that, since their country is providing free education for them (including generous scholarships to study abroad), they have a responsibility to support their country's traditions and policies.

Before the oil boom, Saudi Arabia had a high level of illiteracy. In the 1970s, the Kingdom began to build an impressive array of new schools, ranging from kindergartens to universities, staffed by Saudis and expatriates alike. Except at the kindergarten level, boys and girls may not go to school together.

Boys' schooling is like that in other Arab countries, with kindergarten, primary, intermediate, secondary (high school) and tertiary (university) levels.

63

Saudi girls in a kinder-garten. The opening of a large number of schools for girls reflects the Saudi government's interest in including women in the nation's development process.

After the first year of secondary school, boys may specialize in either scientific or literary studies. There are also vocational schools which offer courses in technical, agricultural and business subjects. Advanced studies take place at numerous colleges and universities, of which the new $3.5 billion Diriyah campus of King Saud University, near Riyadh, is the largest and best known.

The Saudi government will also pay for bright students to study abroad. Most young Saudis who go to college overseas do so in the West. Educational ties between Saudi Arabia and the United States, and to a lesser extent between Saudi Arabia and the United Kingdom, are quite strong.

The first school for girls in Saudi Arabia was set up only in 1956. Before then, if they received any formal education at all, it was from private tutors in their own homes. But education for girls has now become available in every village, town and city. They can learn sciences and languages in addition to Islamic studies. Vocational training and university studies are also open to them. Since they cannot attend classes with men, closed circuit television must be used so that females can listen to male lecturers. Under the policy that women should have separate but equal educational facilities, some all-female campuses have also been built.

THE SPECIAL WORLD OF SAUDI WOMEN

In a dramatic and unexpected move in 1990, a group of 70 veiled Saudi women defied the Kingdom's longstanding policy that women are not allowed to drive cars by driving in a convoy of cars in Riyadh until the police stopped and detained them.

This remarkable demonstration for the right to drive was the first known public protest by Saudi women against the traditional role of women in the country.

Why does Saudi Arabia set what Westerners feel are such severe limitations on the freedom of women? The answer seems to be that in Saudi Arabia one of the most important social values is honor.

The honor of a man himself is inextricably bound up with the honor (chastity) of the women of his family. In comparison with men, women are thought to be weaker and more subject to temptation. Moreover, the rules of behavior are so extremely rigid that a woman can jeopardize her sexual honor merely by talking to or sitting next to a man who is not related to her.

Most working Saudi wo-men are found in the medical, social or edu-cational fields. Here, a Saudi woman monitors a patient via a closed-circuit TV at the King Faisal Hospital and Medical Center.

Once violated, her honor can never be restored. Since the Koran teaches that men have authority over women, it is up to men to make sure that their women do not, even inadvertently, go astray. This is the reason why women are kept in such seclusion—to prevent any stains on the family honor.

The result is that Saudi women are shielded by veil and social convention from all contact with men who are not their close relatives. They are not allowed to go to school with men, to work with men, to drive cars or to appear in public dressed in a "provocative" manner, i.e., without being fully shrouded in a black *abaaya* (cloak). The socially preferred role for Saudi women is to be in the home. They are strongly encouraged to be wives, mothers and homemakers. If women want to or must work, the most appropriate jobs for them are considered to be medical, social or educational work, but only with women or girls as their patients, clients or students.

These restrictions might not be tolerated by women in other societies, but few Saudi women feel they are being treated unfairly. With the solitary exception of the driving episode, their public protests have been virtually nonexistent. The reasons for this are not hard to find.

For one thing, Saudi women have been brought up to accept this way of life as entirely normal and they earn the approval of their husbands and their families if they discharge their duties well. For another, they have virtually no alternative, except to leave the Kingdom and live and work in some other country. And, finally, by conforming to the demands of Saudi society, they are rewarded by a very high degree of personal, social and financial security—so high, in fact, that they might well be envied by other women around the world who do not have such a safety net.

MARRIAGE AND DIVORCE

In Saudi Arabia, men can have up to four wives at a time. The Koran says, however, that if a man feels he cannot treat all his wives with equal fairness, he should take only one. In Mohammed's time, polygamy (having more than one wife) helped the desert tribes survive. Warriors were often killed in battle, leaving women widowed and children fatherless. If men had not been allowed to marry these widows, both the widows and their children might have died.

Some societies, the United States being one of the best examples, put a high value on personal freedom. Men and women are entirely free to marry whomever they like. Traditional societies like Saudi Arabia, on the other hand, look at marriage in a very different light. The Saudis believe the most important question about marriage is not whether a man and a woman will be happy, but whether the marriage will strengthen the two families involved.

Since marriage is much too important to be left to a young man and young woman, almost all marriages are arranged by their parents. Saudis tend to marry young, with girls marrying at 16 to 18 years of age and boys at about 18 to 20. Because marriage is seen as a formal alliance between families, a contract carefully spells out its financial terms. The groom has to pay a "bride price" by giving gold jewelry or other goods to his bride worth an agreed amount of money. These items are the bride's personal property. If the couple divorces, she gets to keep them.

For a man, divorce is very easy. All he has to do is to say "I divorce you" three times. He must then give to the wife whatever is hers under the marriage contract. A woman may also divorce her husband, but this is more difficult to do and requires a divorce order by a religious leader.

It would be considered improper for a girl to show interest in her prospective marriage partner; the general attitude is that love should grow out of marriage, not precede it. Not romantic love, but the proper social arrangements and satisfactory material circumstances are regarded as essential foundations for a successful marriage. Beyond this, parents seek partners for their children who hopefully will prove congenial, but personal compatibility in marriage is thought to be an outcome of fate.

—George A. Lipsky
in Saudi Arabia: Its
People, its Society,
its Culture

WEDDINGS: WOMEN'S WORLD

A young woman almost always accepts as her husband the man her parents have chosen. Her wedding is the most important day in her life and is celebrated elaborately. Wedding expenses are sometimes exorbitant, but the cost is shared by both the husband and the wife's family.

The private, religious part of the wedding is performed separately and before the more public ceremonial events. In Islam, the marriage ceremony itself involves an imam (a religious leader). He meets privately with the bride-to-be and asks her if she will accept the prospective husband. If she agrees, the imam later asks the groom, this time in the presence of four witnesses (who cannot be members of either family) if he will take the woman for his wife. If he says yes, this pronunciation, attested to by the witnesses, makes the marriage valid. The marriage contract is officially recorded by the imam.

At wedding celebrations, held in the evening at the home of the bride or in a hotel, male and female guests do not mix. The men never see the bride, since it is quite unacceptable socially for an unveiled Saudi woman to be seen by men who are not her close relatives. Wedding photos, a new innovation, are taken only by female photographers and are never publicly displayed. The bride and groom make a formal appearance among the women guests to receive their congratulations. Male and female guests bring with them appropriate wedding presents for the new couple.

OLD AGE AND DEATH

The oldest man in a Saudi household is highly respected and has a great deal of power. As the senior male member of the family, he is the court of last appeal and decides what other family members should do to promote the interests of the family as a whole.

The oldest woman, for her part, does not have such a formal decision-making role, but she can exert a powerful behind-the-scenes influence on such critically important family matters as choosing prospective brides or grooms for younger members of the family.

When the senior man is sick or senile, all the other members of the family pool their knowledge and opinions to decide what should be done. The opinions of the senior male are taken into account, too.

After a death, friends of the deceased may pay their condolences by calling on the bereaved family. When Saudis die, they must be buried within 24 hours, a sound policy in such a hot country. The custom is not to have elaborate funeral services or cemeteries, even for very important people. In keeping with the Wahhabi tradition, the grave of King Abdul Aziz had no inscription and was marked only by two flat, upright stones at the head and foot of the burial mound. In 1975, when King Faisal was assassinated by a deranged nephew, he was buried simply and without fanfare in an unmarked grave in the desert. Winds and blowing sand soon erase any trace of a burial in Saudi Arabia.

RELIGION

SAUDI ARABIA is the home of Islam, a religion which was first preached by the Prophet Mohammed during the 7th century A.D. in Mecca and Medina. It has grown enormously since then and is now a major religion with about 700 million believers all over the world. "Islam" in Arabic means "submission" to the will of God. Almost all Saudis are practicing "Moslems," a name which signifies that they believe in Islam.

It would be very hard to exaggerate the importance of religion in Saudi Arabia today. The opening words of all official government documents are the opening words of the Koran: "In the name of Allah, the Compassionate, the Merciful." The very flag of the Kingdom bears the Moslem's declaration of faith, "There is no god but God; Mohammed is the Messenger of God." One of the most common Saudi expressions is "Al Hamdulillah (al HAHM-du-lee-lah), which means "Thanks be to God." No religion but Islam may openly be practiced in Saudi Arabia. And virtually everybody in Saudi Arabia, except for desert travelers, hears the highpitched, melodious early morning call to prayer, issuing in Arabic from loudspeakers at nearby mosques.

Above: **Hajj pilgrims converge on Mecca.**

Opposite: **Pilgrim's tents at Arafat. Situated on a plain ten miles from Mecca, Arafat is the culmination of the hajj. This is where Mohammed preached his last sermon.**

A TOTAL WAY OF LIFE

It is often said that Islam is more than just a religion: it is a total way of life. This is certainly true.

Islam encourages a sense of brotherhood through a shared faith. It provides a set of regulations governing all aspects of family life and offers clear guidelines on personal behavior and legal matters. As a result, devout Moslems feel they can find in Islam the answers to many of the pressing questions of everyday life.

Moreover, in Saudi Arabia there is no clear distinction, as there is the United States and other countries, between "church" (religious activities) and "state" (government projects). The two are deeply intertwined; Saudi Arabia is an Islamic state governed by Islamic law and administered through Islamic social institutions.

THE MATAWAIN

Religious laws and customs in Saudi Arabia are rigidly enforced at the street level and in the *souqs* by the *matawain* ("mah-TAH-wain") or "religious police."

Working for the politically influential "Committee for the Protection of Virtue and the Prevention of Vice," the *matawain* are often older men with henna-dyed beards who carry a small camel whip as a token of office. Semi-educated younger men who reject Western culture are in its ranks, too.

The *matawain* are Islamic fundamentalists whose job is to make sure that stores close promptly at prayer times and that women appearing in public are properly dressed. A woman who is not wearing an ankle-length skirt or whose arms or legs are bare may get a light whipping on her legs or arms from one of the *matawain* to warn her against such "immodest" behavior in the future.

BASIC BELIEFS: GOD AND HUMANITY

Since Saudi Arabia is the cradle of Islam and because this religion is the dominant force in Saudi culture today, it is important to know what Islam teaches. Compared with the fatalistic beliefs it replaced, this new religious code introduced by Mohammed was progressive, generous and enlightened.

ONE GOD Moslems believe there is only one God, who created and sustains the world we live in. Mohammed himself was not divine but was the last and greatest of a series of prophets. In him all earlier prophecies were brought to a final culmination.

PARADISE One of Mohammed's main teachings was that no matter how old you are or what your sins have been, it is never too late to repent. God will judge everybody in terms of their behavior during their lives. Punishments and rewards will be just. Sinners will be cast into the fires of hell. Those whose lives were meritorious, however, will be saved. They will enjoy the pleasures of heaven, which, with its bountiful food and drink, endless streams of pure water and lovely young male and female servants, is just the opposite of the harsh daily life of the desert.

CHARITY Bound together by their common faith, Moslems should ideally be, according to Islam, a caring community united in its submission to God. Islam also stresses the importance of works of charity, for example, easing human suffering and giving money to the poor. Mohammed himself directed that his followers pay special attention to those who were in the greatest need in his own times—women, orphans and slaves. Lending money at interest (usury) is forbidden.

And hold fast, all of you together, to the faith of Allah, and do not separate. And remember Allah's favor unto you: how you were enemies and he made friendship between your hearts so that you became as brothers by his grace...

—a quote from the Koran, III-103

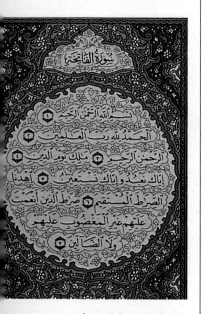

A *surah* from the Koran, the *al-Fatiha*, is recited by devout Moslems every day as part of their prayers.

WRITINGS OF ISLAM

Knowing something about the famous scriptures of Islam—the Koran and the Hadith—also helps us to understand this world religion.

THE KORAN The Koran (also spelled "Qur'an") plays roughly the same central role in Islam as the New Testament does in Christianity, as a divinely-inspired, never-failing source of religious instruction and literary excellence.

The Koran itself is considered by Moslems to be the direct word of God, brought to Mohammed in small increments by the angel Gabriel over a period of 20 years. When Mohammed received these messages from God, he was in a trance. Subsequently, when he recovered from the trance he recited aloud to his followers what had been revealed to him.

Initially recorded by his disciples on whatever materials were conveniently at hand—pieces of paper, stones, palm leaves, bits of leather, camel bones—these recitations were assembled into the Koran, which consists of 114 chapters (called *surahs*) of different lengths. These are known by short catchy titles, for example "The Cow," which refers to creatures or people mentioned in the *surah* itself.

Some of the *surahs* are brief, rhymed, poetic statements. Others are longer and more complex. After the death of Mohammed in A.D. 632, Moslems felt the need for an agreed text of the Koran. Islamic scholars compiled, from different sources and in the purest Arabic, an authoritative text of this sacred book. They succeeded so well that the Koran is considered by virtually all Moslems, and by many non-Moslems as well, to be a religious and literary masterpiece.

THE HADITH With the text of the Koran decided once and for all, scholars could turn their attention to the sayings and traditions surrounding the

Prophet. These are collectively known as the Hadith ("hah-DEETH"), which means a "report" or a record of sayings or traditions. They offer detailed guidance to the faithful on almost all day-to-day activities of life, from how one washes oneself to how to forgive other people.

In the Hadith, tricky moral questions are asked and then cleverly answered. Here is a good example:

A man bought a piece of land and unexpectedly found a pot of gold buried there. Rather than secretly keeping the gold for himself, however, he immediately told the former owner about it. But the former owner, refused to claim the gold, saying that it had not been part of the bargain he had made.

What to do? The solution, proposed by a third man called in to solve the problem, was truly creative: the son of the new owner should marry the daughter of the former owner. In that way, the young couple could then be given the gold as their wedding present!

THE FIVE PILLARS OF ISLAM

After Mohammed died in 632, his followers began to define more formally what it meant to be a Moslem. They identified five key responsibilities for members of the faith. Known as the "Pillars of Islam," these are duties which every Moslem must perform if he or she is able to do so. They include: (1) a declaration of faith, (2) daily prayers, (3) paying a special tax, (4) fasting and (5) a pilgrimage.

DECLARATION OF FAITH To become a Moslem, you must recite aloud a formal profession of faith (the *shahadah*): "There is no god but God; Mohammed is the Messenger of God." This is the first pillar. Once done, this act makes you a member of the believing community and allows you to share fully in its religious creed and its daily way of life.

A cafe is closed for prayer. All offices and shops close for each prayer for up to half an hour.

DAILY PRAYERS Praying five times a day is the second pillar. Believers are urged to pray together with others, but praying alone is also permitted if there is no alternative. The precise time for prayers changes daily, but they are always offered five times a day: before sunrise, in the early afternoon, in the late afternoon, after sunset and then again before going to sleep.

Moslems can pray virtually anywhere, in the mosques, at home, in the desert or at their places of work. In the afternoon, for example, a common sight just outside the supermarkets of Saudi Arabia is a row of men, led by one of their number, who are facing toward Mecca and carrying out in unison the prescribed bows and prostrations of their prayers. Men can pray in the aisle of an airplane, even when the plane is in flight.

Pilgrims pray to God before the Ka'bah, which is draped with a black silk cloth embroidered in gold with verses from the Koran.

Women usually pray at home.

Attendance is encouraged at weekly prayer service which is held at the mosques early on Friday afternoon. Here the imam (the leader of the service) takes a text from the Koran and elaborates on it in what can be a long, emotional sermon.

A SPECIAL TAX The third pillar involves paying a religious tax (*zakat*), which varies from 2.5% to 10%, depending upon the kind of asset being taxed. From a fundamentalist point of view, all Moslems are supposed to pay this tax, but since there are no penalties for failing to do so, in practice it has become a voluntary offering. Revenues raised by the *zakat* are generally used to help the poor.

FASTING The ninth month of the Moslem lunar calendar is known as Ramadan. Fasting during the daylight hours of Ramadan constitutes the fourth pillar. Since there were no clocks in the desert, early Moslems judged the exact time of sunrise as the moment when a white thread could be distinguished from a black one. No eating, drinking, smoking or sexual activities are permitted during the hours of the fast.

THE PILGRIMAGE The fifth and last pillar of Islam is the hajj, the annual pilgrimage to Mecca which every Moslem should make at least once during his or her life if they can afford it. Each year about 1.5 to 2 million Moslems from all over the world converge on Mecca by air, sea and land to participate in one of the world's greatest pilgrimages. When a man has made this pilgrimage, he is entitled to be known by the honorable title of hajji, one who has been on the hajj.

RITES OF THE HAJJ

There are two kinds of pilgrimage to Mecca, Islam's most sacred city. These are the shorter *umrah* (visit), which can be done at any time of year, and the hajj itself, which has a more elaborate ritual and which takes place only once a year. The rites of the hajj require about 12 days to complete, but many pilgrims stay on longer to visit the other holy city, Medina.

As a first step of the hajj, before entering Mecca, the pilgrims put on

Pilgrims collect pebbles in order to perform the ritual stoning of Satan, which takes the form of throwing the stones at symbolic pillars.

special clothes signifying their holy state and their equality before God. For a man this outfit consists of unsewn white toweling and unsewn sandals; the only requirement for a woman is that she is not veiled. The pilgrims must also chant to God, showing acceptance of the rituals which lie ahead.

Entering the Grand Mosque of Mecca, the pilgrim walks seven times around the Ka'bah, in which is set the Black Stone, a sacred relic believed by the faithful to date from the time of Adam. Pilgrims kiss or gesture toward the stone. Other rites include drinking from the Well of Zamzam, a ritualized running (more like a brisk walk) between two low hills, and having one's head shaved or one's hair cut.

The culmination of the hajj, however, is the Standing on the Plain of Arafat, where pilgrims stand all afternoon reading from the Koran and repeating the prayer, "Here I am, O God, here I am!" The next day they gather pebbles, which they throw at stone pillars with Islam's famous cry, "*Allahu Akbar*" ("God is most great!"). Casting the stones symbolizes the casting out of evil. Sheep are sacrificed and the meat is given to the poor.

The Prophet's Mosque in Medina is adorned with exquisite minarets and has 10 major gates. It houses the Prophet's chamber which contains the graves of the Prophet himself and those of his companions.

THE GREAT MOSQUES OF THE KINGDOM

From very modest beginnings the great mosques of Saudi Arabia—the Quba Mosque near Medina, the Prophet's Mosque in Medina and the Grand Mosque of Mecca—have evolved into a blaze of glory. They are at the same time places of prayer and centers for education and discussion.

Because Moslems in Saudi Arabia are strongly encouraged to pray five times a day, mosques were traditionally built where most people congregated, in the middle of towns or near markets. Mosques vary in size and architectural design, but they have similar parts. The outer courtyard can also be used for prayers if the mosque itself is crowded. There is also an inner area designed for worship.

Since Moslems are to pray facing the Ka'bah in Mecca, a prayer niche, a recess in the mosque, shows the direction of Mecca. On Friday, sermons are given from a high pulpit inside the mosque. The melodious, ethereal call to prayer is made from a tall minaret overlooking the mosque. In the

past, the call was made by a muzzein ("mu-ZAIN") with a far-reaching voice. Today, the muzzein uses loudspeakers instead.

The Quba Mosque, Islam's first mosque, was built by Mohammed in A.D. 622 when he moved from Mecca to Medina. It has been upgraded many times, most recently by King Fahd in 1986. In Medina, Mohammed also built a second mosque which is named after him, the Prophet's Mosque. It, too, has been improved many times. In the late 1800s, for example, a lovely prayer hall and ornate colonnades were added.

Impressive as these two mosques are, however, the Grand Mosque of Mecca is the spiritual heart of Islam. It contains the Ka'bah, a cubic stone structure about 45 feet high and 30 feet wide, which is located in the center of the mosque. A huge black silk cloth, the Kiswah, is embroidered in gold with verses from the Koran. It is draped over the Ka'bah and is replaced every year. Flanked by minarets 270 feet high and often renewed and expanded, the Grand Mosque is a masterpiece of Islamic taste, craftsmanship and design.

Located in the center of Mecca, the Grand Mosque has been rebuilt and enlarged several times, and is today spacious enough to accommodate 600,000 worshipers.

LANGUAGE

ALL SAUDIS speak Arabic, which is a Semitic language related to Hebrew and Aramaic. Arabic is one of the half a dozen widely used international languages today, spoken by over 120 million people over a large area including North Africa, most of the Arabian Peninsula and parts of the Middle East.

Many Saudis believe that Arabic has a special importance because it is the language of the Koran. The verbal richness of the Koran has, for the Saudis, set a world standard for literary elegance. The wide range of subtle meanings which Arabic can express makes this language especially well-suited to poetry.

Arabic has two basic forms. The first is classical (written or literary) Arabic which is the same throughout the whole Arab world. The second, spoken Arabic, varies considerably from one region to another. Translating Arabic words into other languages is quite difficult because the sound system of Arabic is very different from English and other European languages. Moreover, some of the sounds commonly used in Arabic are never used in Western languages.

As a result, there are several legitimate ways in English to spell the same Arabic word. For example, "Moslem" and "Muslim" are both correct. "Mohammed" can also be spelled "Muhammad," "Muhamid" and "Mohammad." The House of "Saud" might be more accurately referred to as the House of "Sa'ood." One author found no fewer than 16 different spellings, all acceptable, for the Red Sea port of "Jeddah."

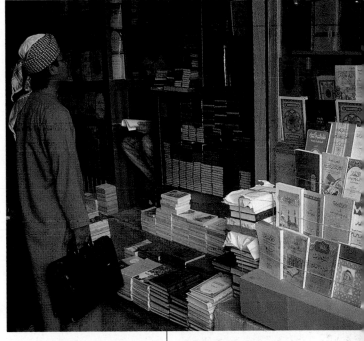

Above: **A bookshop sells Islamic literature. The expressive Arabic language is the vehicle of Islam and is an important cultural legacy of the Peninsula.**

Opposite: **A sculpture in Jeddah is inspired by Arabic calligraphy.**

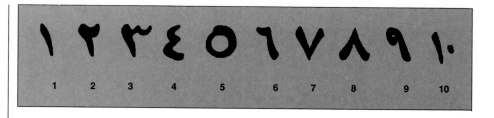

١	٢	٣	٤	٥	٦	٧	٨	٩	١٠
1	2	3	4	5	6	7	8	9	10

Right: Arabic numerals, as we know them today, were borrowed from the Arabs, who got them from the Hindus of India centuries ago. Later, the Arabs developed a different numeric system. The picture shows the numbers that are used in the Arabic world today and our present-day Arabic numerals.

Below: Arabic calligraphy with the words, "In the name of Allah, the Compassionate, the Merciful."

THE ARABIC ALPHABET, CALLIGRAPHY AND NUMBERS

The Arabic alphabet was probably invented in the 4th century A.D. Thanks to the rapid advance of the Arab empire after the death of Mohammed, it spread quickly and is now the second most widely used alphabet in the world (the Latin alphabet is the most common).

The Arabic alphabet has 28 letters and is written and read from the right hand side of the page to the left hand side. The earliest copies of the Koran were written in a heavy, monumental script known as Kufic. About A.D. 1000, however, this style was replaced by Naskhi, a lighter script which is widely used in Saudi Arabia today. The form of this script is cursive, which is a flowing style of writing which joins letters together.

In Saudi Arabia and other Islamic countries, calligraphy is a highly valued art because it is often used to copy the Koran, which Moslems believe contains the very words of God. Calligraphers writing in Arabic use a reed pen with an angled point. This point lets them make bold downstrokes, narrow upstrokes and all the variations between these extremes.

Kufic, Naskhi and other regional scripts lend themselves extraordinarily well to a splendid calligraphy, whether written on paper or employed to adorn the walls of mosques and other buildings. In these latter cases, verses from the Koran are often carved into the walls or written on tiles, which are then glazed and set in the walls.

Many English words come from Arabic such as alchemy, alcohol, algebra, alkali, almanac, arsenal, assassin, azimuth, cipher, elixir, nadir, mosque, sugar, syrup and zero. The numbers 0, 1, 2, 3, 4, 5, 6, 7, 8, 9, so familiar to us, are known as Arabic numerals. The Arabs initially learned them from the Indians and later passed them on to the West.

A group of Saudi boys pose for a picture. Saudi children are usually named a few days or weeks after birth.

PERSONAL NAMES

Saudis may give a boy as many as four names: his own name, his father's and grandfather's names, and a tribal or family name.

There is a wide range of personal names. Some typical names for Bedouin men are Khalaf, Sattam, Nayif, Mit'ib and Rakan; for Bedouin women, Sitih, Wadha, Joza, Amsha and Salma. Among the settled (non-Bedouin) Saudis, men's names include Salim, Salman, Nasir, Salih and Saif; women's include Miznih, Hissih, Haya, Mudi and Zainab.

There are no family names as such among the nomads. Each man takes the name of his clan or tribe as his last name. Examples of such names are Al Harbi, Al Shammari and Al Marri. Among the settled Saudis, however, family names are the rule, for example, Al Gublan, Al Jabir and Al Bassam. ("Al" in this context means "dynasty" or "house of." Thus "Al Saud" is the House of Saud, i.e., the royal family.)

In practice, not all a person's names are used. A man might be known as Mohammed bin Ahmad Al Sudairi—"Mohammed the son of Ahmad of the Sudairi family." A woman takes her father's name and before marriage might be known as Nura bint Khalid, "Nura the daughter of Khalid." When she marries, she will take her husband's name. If she bears a son, she will be known as *umm* ("mother of"), followed by the name of her son, i.e. *umm* Ali ("the mother of Ali").

BODY LANGUAGE

Within the circle of their extended family and with friends of their own sex, Saudis are warm, smiling, open people. Saudi men greet each other enthusiastically and often hold hands while walking together along a street. (This only shows their friendship for each other; it does not have any sexual overtones.) But in the presence of strangers, Saudis are usually more restrained and are not given to public displays of emotion.

When he shakes hands, a Saudi man prefers a short limp handshake rather than a long, bone-crushing grip. After shaking hands with another Saudi, he may briefly touch his right hand to his heart to show his sincerity.

If he is meeting another Arabic speaker, he will probably greet him with the traditional welcome, "is-salam alaykum" ("is-saal-laam a-LAY-kum," which means "peace be upon you"). The traditional response is "wa-alaykum is-salam" ("and to you be peace").

Men and women move in totally separate social circles when they are outside the extended family. When a husband and wife go to a party, the husband will join the men in one part of the house. The woman joins the other women in a different room. Outside their own homes, Saudi men and women never mix and mingle with the opposite sex.

Saudis enjoy being hospitable and friendly to one another.

Public displays of affection between men and women, even between husband and wife, are strictly forbidden. The *matawain* (religious police) can arrest couples who are holding hands or otherwise touching each other in public.

THE MEDIA: PRESS, RADIO AND TELEVISION

The press, radio and TV comes under the control of the government of Saudi Arabia. There are several daily and weekly Arabic newspapers.

Aware of the basic role played by the information media in encouraging participation in development projects and in educating the citizens about their responsibilities and national duty, the government has made ample provisions for radio and television services. Programs now reach 90% of the country's population. Many of the programs are religious and literary in nature.

The government does not tolerate any criticism of Islam and "pornography" such as advertisements showing women models wearing bras or panties are prohibited.

LANGUAGES OTHER THAN ARABIC

Because of Saudi Arabia's long relationship with Britain and the United States, English is widely spoken by educated Saudis, military officers and by some merchants in the major *souqs* or traditional markets. There are also English language schools, newspapers and radio and TV programs.

Many of the foreign workers in the Kingdom do not speak Arabic but do speak at least some English. As a result, since the 1970s it has become the lingua franca (common tongue) of business, aviation, medicine, transportation and communications.

Recognizing the media as a powerful tool for change, the Saudi government has set up the Riyadh Television Complex to bring informative programming to 90% of the country's population.

ARTS

MOSQUES AND POETRY are Saudi Arabia's two important contributions to the arts of the world. Other forms of Saudi art have been severely restricted by a principle of art technically known as "aniconism"—which means a prohibition, for religious reasons, of representing any living creature by painting, sculpture or other means. Because of this prohibition, artists in Saudi Arabia have not been free, as artists in other countries usually have been, to create portraits or drawings of people or animals.

This prohibition stems from an Islamic belief that only God can create life. According to the conservative Saudi interpretation of this belief, an artist who produces an image of a living creature is considered to be trying to act like God. Moreover, Saudi conservatives have also feared that the images themselves might become idols. In other words, people might begin to focus too much of their attention on a painting, a carving or some other image rather than on God himself. To avoid any danger of idolatry, art in Saudi Arabia has traditionally been confined to abstract, symbolic forms.

Above: **Automobiles protude from a huge concrete cube in Jeddah—an imaginative blend of art and technology.**

Opposite: **Elegant fish sculpture lends a modern touch to Jeddah's Corniche area near the sea, which has been transformed into a recreation center.**

89

In practice, other Moslem countries have not always followed rigorously the guiding principle of aniconism, but Saudi Arabia has always taken an uncompromising stand. Purists there have frowned not only on representational art but also on large-scale public presentations of drama, fiction, singing or instrumental music. As a result, the intellectual side of Saudi life has been dominated by the spoken and written word and by Islam.

The nomadic life of the Saudis also imposed its own strict logistical limitations on art since a Bedouin could own only what he could carry on his camel. Even if representational art had been tolerated or even encouraged, transporting paintings, drawings or carvings from one grazing ground to another, on camels, year in and year out, would not have been practical.

A Saudi basket vendor displays his colorful wares. Made of palm fronds, the baskets are woven by hand.

THE FUNCTIONAL ROLE OF THE ARTS

Given the prohibition on representational art, traditional Saudi artisans turned their attention instead to making everyday functional objects more beautiful. In this they succeeded, despite the limited natural resources at their disposal. Objects in daily use were carefully made and were decorated with geometric, floral and calligraphic designs.

Handsome wooden incense burners perfumed tents and houses with the smoke of frankincense.

Graceful brass water jugs were used to rinse the right hand before eating. Roasted coffee beans and cardamon seeds were pounded in sturdy, elegant brass mortars. The resulting mixture was boiled in nicely decorated brass coffeepots. Big wooden trays three feet in diameter were used to serve mutton and rice at banquets. Chests, bowls, saddle frames and other items made of wood were embellished with brass or silver nails. Prayer beads, made from materials gathered from around the world, were traded in Mecca. House doors were ornately carved with geometric designs. Narrow-necked pottery urns stored water or food. Decorated leather goods, mats and baskets, all well-suited to the tasks at hand, were also produced.

One unavoidable casualty of the modernization of Saudi Arabia in recent years has been traditional handicrafts. In many cases, handmade items have been replaced by cheaper mass-produced substitutes imported from abroad. Fortunately, however, many old pieces are still in daily use. Others can be found for sale at the *souqs*.

Poetry and storytelling have long been part of the Saudi oral tradition. In the desert, under the night sky, men would sit around a campfire and narrate verses and stories celebrating romance, war and the fate of humankind.

POETS OF THE DESERT

Since pre-Islamic days, poetry has been considered the highest form of art in the Arabian Peninsula. One reason may be that the harshness of nomadic life could be softened by beautiful words and phrases. Another reason is that the ban on fictional writing (banned because fiction, as something "untrue," seemed too close to lying) gave rise to a tradition of intentional verbal exaggeration and overstatement. This became a well-accepted way to carry listeners beyond the here-and-now reality without at the same time getting them involved in direct lies.

The tradition of exaggeration blended in well with the nomads' love of poetry. With their vivid imaginations, they did not draw a sharp distinction in their lyric poetry between the real and the unreal. Words became their favorite form of artistic expression. To be a poet was to hold a post of great honor. According to an eleventh century Moslem writer, whenever a poet emerged in an Arab tribe, the other tribes would come and offer congratulations, for the poet was a defense to their honor, a protection for their good repute. He immortalized their deeds of glory, and published their eternal fame.

It is almost impossible to translate this kind of poetry adequately into English, but here are some lines from a famous love poem in which a man describes his beloved:

Out I brought her, and as she stepped she trailed behind us to cover our footsteps the skirt of an embroidered gown ...
At eventide she lightens the black shadows, as if she were the lamp kindled in the night of a monk at his devotions.

In the poverty of desert life, a man who could string words together in mystical chains which sang to the heart rather than the mind was indeed a man deserving of praise.

STORYTELLING AND LITERATURE

The Saudis have always been great storytellers. Sometimes Saudi men will go out into the desert, roast sheep on a campfire and tell stories far into the night. Tales of valor in battle are especially valued and are told and retold. In recent years, however, this oral tradition has been dying out. Now, thanks to the spread of education, most Saudis can read. Passing on stories by word of mouth is therefore no longer the only way they can communicate.

There are literary clubs at institutions of higher learning. As writers, the Saudis have the freest hand when they turn to poetry. The prestigious King Faisal Award annually recognizes achievements in the humanities and sciences. All literary and scientific output, however, must conform to the religious establishment's strict interpretation of Islam.

WEAVING AND EMBROIDERY

If poetry was a man's job, weaving and embroidery were part of the nomadic woman's world. One of the biggest tasks for women was making the long Bedouin tent. Known as "houses of hair," these tents were woven by hand from narrow strips made of goat, sheep or camel hair. On the outside they were black (goat hair in Arabia is jet-black), but the interior was decorated with rich geometric patterns. Colorful woven curtains separated the tent into three sections: one for guests, where they were served coffee; another as a living space for family members and a store-room for supplies; and the third as a cooking area.

Other woven items were also essential to nomadic life. Women made highly-decorated riding litters, saddle bags and tasseled blankets to use when traveling on camels. Woolen cloaks kept out the winter cold. Dresses were made from hand-loomed textiles. Carpets formed a floor for the tent, kept the sand at bay and added touches of vivid color to the monochrome brown of desert life.

Embroidery was traditionally a skill learned by all young women. In the past almost all clothing in the Arabian Peninsula was embroidered by hand. Since the invention of the sewing machine, hand embroidery has given way to machine work.

The huge Kiswah (the ornate black cloth draped over the Ka'bah), which was formerly made in Egypt every year and presented to Saudi Arabia, is the biggest, most important embroidered item now produced in the Kingdom. Each year, a new Kiswah is made by skilled embroiderers using gold and silver metal thread on black velvet. The exquisite, flowing calligraphy from the Koran is surrounded by interlaced patterns of leaves.

Opposite: **A *souq* or traditional market in Jeddah sells a variety of goods from mats to copper and brass ware and embroidered clothing.**

Below: **Carpet merchants. Carpets were first used as coverings for earthern floors and were the only form of decorative art practiced by nomadic people.**

BEDOUIN JEWELRY

In a nomadic society without banks and with few material possessions, a woman's wealth was in her jewelry. A Bedouin woman received most of her jewelry when she was married. Usually made from silver studded with turquoise and red stones, it was melted down at her death, to be recast later as new pieces in the same traditional designs.

Among these designs are ornate necklaces, bracelets, armlets, anklets, belts, nose and ear ornaments, and finger-rings and toe-rings. These are still made in Saudi Arabia by silversmiths using techniques which have not changed much for hundreds of years. Metal is annealed (heated and then gradually cooled it to make it soft and malleable), fused, cast, hammered, embossed or engraved. Silver jewelry is often ornamented with filigree work—thin wire twisted into delicate patterns and soldered into place.

New jewelry is sold by the weight of its silver and stones, not by its workmanship. Imported machine-made items, being much cheaper to manufacture than handmade Bedouin jewelry, have in recent years been pricing traditional jewelry out of the market. Nevertheless, a good deal of used traditional jewelry is still available in the *souqs* of Riyadh. Bargaining for it is a favorite pastime of many expatriates.

ORNATE WEAPONS

Because of the insecurity of desert life, men in Saudi Arabia were, until recent times, heavily armed. Spears, well-tempered swords and camel-hide shields were carried before rifles became widely available as a result of World War I.

When weapons were no longer needed for personal defense they were still carried for ceremonial and cultural reasons. A man felt naked without at least a dagger at his waist. This profusion of weapons offered unlimited opportunities for ornamentation and decoration. Silversmiths devoted themselves to embossing the hilts of swords and daggers. Sheaths for daggers received meticulous attention. Traditionally made of wood and encased in leather or cloth, they were finished with silver and semi-precious stones and carried in embroidered belts. Fine center-fire rifles from the West were engraved and decorated with gold. Traditional Arabian muzzle-loading rifles had graceful, curving wooden stocks often studded with brass decorations.

THE ARDHA (SWORD DANCE)

The *ardha* is a traditional but unstructured Arabian dance performed in public places on religious and festive occasions.

The dancers (all men) are dressed in flowing white robes and are armed with long swords. They stamp heavily and flash their swords, hopping from one foot to another, in time to the African-like rhythms of accompanying drums and tambourines.

As part of the performance, young girls under 12 years old "ululate" (this means they utter high-pitched, wordless wailings). Wearing long bright dresses, they sway in time to the music and flick their long hair (which is heavily ornamented with beads) from side to side.

The audience may clap along or even join in the dance. When male members of the royal family are present they sometimes join the *ardha* dancers, too. When they do, they not only enjoy themselves, but they pay public tribute to the memory of how their ancestor, King Abdul Aziz, won Saudi Arabia—by the sword.

ARCHITECTURE: TRADITIONAL AND MODERN

The most dramatic ancient ruins in Saudi Arabia are the well-preserved tombs and buildings carved into solid rock at Madain Salih in the northwest part of the country. These are more than two thousand years old and

A traditional house in Riyadh with an enclosed yard. Windows and air vents allow air to circulate into the house.

were built by the Nabateans, a long-vanished people who once prospered as middlemen in the Arabian Peninsula's spice trade.

During the early years of Islam architecture was simple and functional. Mosques began as minimal structures and only later did they evolve into their present glories. In the past only the rich had houses made of stone. The less fortunate had to be content with homes made of sun-dried mud bricks, which were cheap to make, easy to repair and kept dwellings cool in the summer and warm in the winter. Roof structures were usually made of tamarisks.

Traditional architecture characterizes this house in Jeddah. The use of slatted wooden shutters and screens ensures privacy while permitting cool breezes to pass through.

Thick-walled forts and palaces were also made of these coarse, sun-baked mud bricks which are durable and strong. The historic fortified palace in Riyadh, Qasr al-Masmak, which Abdul Aziz captured in 1902, is a good example.

The old houses of Jeddah were quite remarkable. Two to four stories high, their windows and balconies were protected by elaborately carved wooden screens, which provided both privacy and ventilation. Ladies could sit in proper seclusion behind these screens and still see what was going on in the narrow streets below. In the wetter Asir region, pieces of slate were set at an angle into whitewashed walls to protect them from hail and rain.

The rapid development of Saudi Arabia since the oil boom has resulted in a large number of modern buildings in which traditional Saudi styles and modern materials are combined. This successful integration is best exemplified by many of the ministries, official buildings and other building complexes in Riyadh today. One of the most striking is the Royal Pavilion at the King Khalid International Airport. Another successful blending of old and new is the United Nations building and the spectacular International Stadium.

LEISURE

FOR SAUDIS most entertainment takes place in the home and involves the family and relatives. There is not much public entertainment in Saudi Arabia. There are no pubs or bars because alcohol is banned. Saudi men and women are not supposed to mix socially, which rules out movies, restaurants, plays, art museums and many other cultural activities that adults of both sexes might conceivably attend.

Spending time with one's own family, keeping in close touch with other members of the extended family, celebrating birthdays, arranging marriages, catching up on the latest family gossip and choosing and watching films and videos—these are the favorite Saudi pastimes. Some Saudis participate in sports, and those who can afford it take wonderful vacation trips to countries with a cooler climate.

Left: **Like their desert ancestors, modern Saudis attach a great deal of importance to the family. Most of their leisure time is spent with other family members.**

Opposite: **Young camel riders receive their prizes at a camel race. A yearly event, the camel race attracts hundreds of spectators, including members of the royal family.**

TRADITIONAL SPORTS

The major sports of the Saudis, during the days when most of them were nomads, were all related to the desert. Favorite traditional sports today include camel racing, horseracing and falconry.

The Bedouins loved to hold occasional camel races. This tradition is still perpetuated by the royal family in the annual King's Camel Race, staged by the National Guard in the desert near the Riyadh airport. In a creative blend of old and new that is typical of Saudi Arabia today, the Bedouins bring their camels to the racecourse sandwiched into the backs of their little Toyota pickup trucks. The race itself is very demanding. It covers about 10 miles of desert and takes roughly two hours to complete. The riders can be quite young—boys do well at this sport—and receive prizes from the King himself if they finish in one of the top five places.

A camel is transported to the racecourse by a Toyota pickup truck, ensuring that the camel arrives fresh and ready to race.

THE CAMEL

In the past camels were used by the nomads chiefly for carrying their tents and their families from one grazing area to another.

An Arabian camel is very hardy and well-adapted to desert life. It does not begin to sweat until its blood temperature has risen considerably. It does not loose much water when it urinates. If there is enough moisture in the herbs and grass it eats (i.e., in the winter), a camel can go for one week without additional water. During the summer, however, when the sun is hotter and the grazing dry, it needs to drink every two or three days.

Female camels are the best for nomadic life. They produce a nutritious milk—which the Bedouins drink—for almost half a year after giving birth. They are more docile than male camels and can therefore be used for riding. And, last but not least, they have more endurance than the males. For all these reasons, female camels are preferred. Male camels are generally killed for their meat when they are still young. The older males are used to carry the tents and other camping gear.

A horse is being led to the track at the Equestrian Club in Riyadh. Horseracing is another popular traditional sport and many of the horses are owned by Saudi princes.

Horseracing is also popular. The desert's great heat, lack of water and limited grazing made it difficult and expensive to keep horses. Perhaps because of this, they have become a real status symbol. The royal family itself enjoys horseracing. Some of the princes enter their own thoroughbreds in the races held near Riyadh. Crown Prince Abdullah has long had a passionate interest in horses and horsemanship and has served as the chairman of Riyadh's luxurious Equestrian Club. There is no legal betting at horse-races, but the sport is quite popular with princes and public alike.

To conserve Saudi Arabia's wildlife, hunting with firearms has been banned since 1977, but falcons are still used to hunt birds (particularly the bustard, a big bird, now rare in Saudi Arabia, which runs along the ground) and rabbits. The training of falcons requires patience and skill and several weeks of arduous work.

THE ARABIAN HORSE

According to a Bedouin legend, "Allah created, of a handful of mud, a horse of a chestnut color, like gold, and said to the horse, 'Thou shalt have station and power above all things and beasts that are subject to man.' "

This lovely creation, the Arabian horse, has lived in the Arabian Peninsula since 5,000 B.C. Over the centuries, selective breeding has resulted in a remarkable animal of exceptional beauty, speed, intelligence, endurance, gentleness and strength.

Arabian horses are also remarkably prepotent. This means that they cross well with all other breeds and pass on to their offspring their own genes—the units of inheritance which determine such traits as the speed, color and physical conformation of a horse.

Modern thoroughbred horses in the United States and other countries now carry the genes of the famous Arabian horses of the past. Three of the most well-known of these Arabians, named after their British owners, were the Godolphin Arabian (born about 1725), the Darley Arabian (born about 1688) and the Byerley Turk (born about 1690). These three horses alone have contributed nearly 27% of the genes which make today's thoroughbreds so beautiful and so fast.

Arabian horses are now bred not only in Saudi Arabia, especially in the Najd, but in many other countries around the world. They excel as riding horses, particularly in the fast-growing sport of long distance riding.

The falconer and falcon. In the old days, falcons were used to hunt game for food by the desert nomads. Today, this method of hunting has developed into a sport.

During the hunt itself, the falcon is hooded and perches on the falconer's forearm, which is protected from the bird's talons by a heavy leather glove. When the prey is seen, the falcon is unhooded and sent aloft. With its keen eyesight, it quickly spots and attacks the prey, diving at it with sharp talons fully extended. The falcon stays with its catch until the keeper arrives. He rewards it with a tiny bit of meat and then hoods it again. Falcons live up to 15 years, but they are at their best as hunters during the first five years.

MODERN SPORTS

Getting and staying in good physical condition is not a national preoccupation in Saudi Arabia. The dry heat in the interior of the country and the high humidity along the coasts make outdoor activity something that most Saudis try to avoid during the day when they stay out of the sun if they can. Even those who like to engage in sports find the going difficult. During the heat of the day it is nearly impossible to play exhausting games such as soccer. Moreover, in the extreme dryness, it is very hard to keep any kind of playing field green enough for even early morning or evening games; so difficult, in fact, that, in Jeddah, golfers must play on a small dusty golf course which has putting greens made of oiled sand rather than grass.

Modern track facilities, such as this in Riyadh, are encouraging more and more young Saudis to participate in sports.

An indoor swimming pool in a sports complex in Riyadh. Sports complexes are found in the major cities of Saudi Arabia to provide facilities for international competitions, training and recreation. They also serve as a cultural meeting place for the population at large.

Despite these limitations there is a growing interest in both individual and team sports, especially among Saudi students. Especially through its Organization for Youth Welfare, the Saudi government has showed its commitment to introducing modern sports to the Kingdom. Basketball has become popular. Facilities for martial arts have been built. The polished tile floors of the Nassariya Gate, a public monument in Riyadh, have proved ideal for learning how to roller-skate. Most major cities and universities now have swimming pools, athletic fields, tracks and other facilities for sports. Even though few Saudis feel completely at home in the water, power boating, sailing, water skiing and jet skiing have caught on in Jeddah.

Some Saudis also like to participate in the sports enjoyed by many of the Western expatriates in the country. These include tennis, horseback riding, camping and rally driving in the desert, boating, fishing, snorkeling and scuba diving in the Red Sea.

SOCCER

By far the most popular team sport is soccer, which is played informally in open spaces in the cities and more formally in big stadiums. Soccer draws eager crowds and is enthusiastically supported by members of the royal family. The new International Sports Stadium in Riyadh is built around a soccer field and has a capacity of 67,000 spectators. The Saudis have hired well-known soccer coaches to bring their teams up to international standards. Working with these experts, young Saudi players are learning the importance of hard and continued training, punctuality and self-discipline. A national Football Federation has also been set up to encourage soccer and to promote the official Saudi soccer team, which performed well at the 1984 Olympic Games in Los Angeles.

A Saudi soccer team poses for a picture.

FESTIVALS

SAUDI ARABIA has two nationwide seasons of merrymaking each year. Both of these holidays, which are known as the Eids ("EEds"), are important religious and family celebrations.

One other day is commemorated officially, the Saudi National Day, which marks the unification of the kingdom of Saudi Arabia in 1932.

The Saudis do not celebrate the birthday of the Prophet Mohammed nor do they hold regional festivals. In their private lives, however, they do celebrate other family events such as the birth of a child (especially a boy) and weddings.

THE TWO EIDS

The first of the two annual national holidays, Eid al-Fitr ("The Feast of the Breaking of the Fast"), is also known as Eid al-Sagghir ("The Feast of the Little Festival"). It celebrates the end of the difficult, demanding, month-long Ramadan fast. Going without food or drink during the long, hot hours of the desert day, from sunrise to sunset, is never an easy matter. As a result, the end of the Ramadan fast is a time of real happiness and rejoicing.

The exact date of this Eid is never known precisely in advance because it depends on the proper sighting of the moon the night before the festival begins. Sometimes the Eid is announced after midnight, after the children have gone to bed. This gives the celebration a great deal of suspense for them.

Opposite: **Children are dressed in their best on Eid al-Fitr, which celebrates the end of the fasting month.**

Below: **Mosques are crowded on religious holidays such as the Eids. Besides visiting friends and relatives, Moslem families visit the mosques to pray and give thanks.**

111

During the Eid holidays, Saudi families also take their children on outings, such as this trip to an amusement park in Jeddah.

The Eid al-Fitr holiday itself officially lasts for three days, when all government and most business offices are closed. In practice, however, much of government and professional life in Saudi Arabia gradually slows down to a near-halt as Eid al-Fitr approaches. This pronounced pause in official and business activity usually lasts for about three weeks—one week before the celebration, one week for the holiday itself and one week after Eid al-Fitr.

Eid al-Fitr is a religious event but at the same time it is very much a family holiday, in some ways like the American Thanksgiving or Christmas. Although Saudi Arabia is now changing rapidly and each family may not follow the same customs, the traditional way of celebrating Eid al-Fitr is still observed by many Saudis.

These families get up early and gather together for a quick snack of dates and coffee. This is the first daytime meal taken since the Ramadan fast began. Then it is time for prayers. Fathers take their families to the mosque. Because of the big crowds celebrating this holiday, Eid prayers are offered not only at small neighborhood mosques but also in very large mosques or on specially consecrated grounds.

After prayers, family members welcome the end of the long fast by greeting each other and their neighbors with the salutation, "Happy Eid!", much as Americans wish each other "Merry Christmas" and "Happy New Year." Then Saudi families enjoy a special big breakfast. Children love Eid al-Fitr. They not only get new clothes but also Eid presents of candy and money. Both the children and their parents look forward to a traditional sweet, pink, apricot drink with which they can break the Ramadan fast.

After breakfast families go from house to house visiting each other, the younger married members of the family (sons) calling on the elder members (their fathers). A sheep is slaughtered and cooked for a big lunch hosted by the senior member of the family. In recent years, some amusement parks have opened in Saudi cities and parents often take their young children there during the Eid holidays.

The other Eid is Eid al-Adha ("The Feast of the Sacrifice"), also known as Eid al-Kabir ("The Feast of the Big Festival"). It celebrates the end of the hajj and commemorates Abraham's submission to God, a submission dramatically shown by Abraham's willingness to sacrifice to God his own son, Ishmael.

This Eid is also a joyful time because Moslems feel a profound sense of thanksgiving and accomplishment when they have participated in the hajj. Although the pace of life slows down for Eid al-Adha, this four-day holiday is not celebrated with quite the same sense of excitement as Eid al-Fitr. However, it, too, centers on the extended family. A lamb is slaughtered, a big family meal is prepared and food or alms are given to the poor.

THE SAUDI NATIONAL DAY

The Saudi National Day celebrates the uniting of the country under the name of Saudi Arabia. Technically this is not a holiday because there are no parades or other public events and people are still expected to go to work. The focal point of the national day is the public release of the King's formal address to his Council of Ministers. Important new government policies, however, are not announced in this speech and its release is usually a pro forma (for the record) event.

LIST OF OFFICIAL HOLIDAYS

The dates for the following two holidays, Eid al-Fitr, the breaking of the fast of Ramadan, and Eid al-Adha, the culmination of the Hajj, vary according to the lunar calendar.

Saudi National Day always falls on September 23. This is the only official holiday that is not observed according to the Islamic calendar.

DIVIDING UP THE YEAR: THE LUNAR CALENDAR

With the exception of the National Day, which is always held on September 23, Saudi holidays do not occur on the same day each year. This is because the Saudis use a lunar calendar to calculate them, rather than the Gregorian calendar common to most of the world.

A lunar year is composed of 12 months, which vary between 29 and 30 days. Since a lunar year is 10 or 11 days shorter than a Gregorian year, it does not correspond with the Gregorian calendar that we use today. This fact directly affects Saudi life. The Ramadan fast, for example, moves forward 10 or 11 days each year. Sometimes it occurs in the cooler winter months and sometimes in the blazing heat of summer.

The Saudi Royal Band performs at a state function.

CHRISTMAS IN THE DESERT

Although the public practice of any religion other than Islam is not permitted in Saudi Arabia, it is a mark of Saudi tolerance that foreigners are allowed to celebrate the Christmas season openly. Many of them do so with great enthusiasm.

In Jeddah, for example, expatriates bring Christmas trees, both big and small, back with them when they fly to the Kingdom from the United States or Europe. Christmas decorations appear on their houses, Christmas cards are exchanged and turkeys are served at Christmas dinners.

FOOD

SAUDI ARABIANS like to eat well. Whether they are sitting on chairs and eating Western-style food with knife and fork, or squatting on the floor eating a traditional feast of mutton and rice with their fingers, the big serving table will be groaning with delicious foods.

At a meal, offering several different kinds of food in great quantity is considered good manners. So is setting the table nicely, if possible with elegant silver utensils, and decorating it with bowls of fresh fruit. This lavish hospitality shows the generosity of the host and hostess and their concern for the welfare of their family or guests.

One food and one beverage, however, are strictly forbidden to Saudis: pork, because it comes from pigs, which are considered unclean, and alcohol, which Moslems are not supposed to drink.

Opposite: **A public fish market. Fish is a source of protein available to Saudi Arabians, besides lamb and beef. Pork is forbidden to Moslems.**

Below: **A typical Saudi dish consisting of rice with ground lamb and nuts.**

TYPICAL MEALS

Saudis who have been educated in or who have traveled to the West may prefer to sit on chairs and to use knives, forks and spoons, rather than sitting on rugs and using their right hand to eat. They serve both Middle Eastern and Western food, often at the same meal. And since virtually all Saudis of middle class or higher status have servants, at minimum, a male cook (usually an Egyptian, Sudanese or Yemeni), they do not have to worry about cooking and cleaning up. The modern kitchens in the homes of these Saudis will be very similar to state-of-the-art kitchens in the United States.

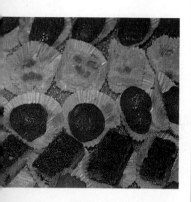

Made from semolina or rice flour, *halva* come with different fillings. Some might be filled with dried fruits such as dates, figs and apricots, others with chopped nuts or sesame seeds.

Typical Saudi dishes include *shikamba* (a creamy lamb soup with meat balls in it); a fruit and vegetable salad made with apples, dates, walnuts, lettuce, mayonnaise, yoghurt and lemon juice; spinach and meat *kofta* (spinach, ground lamb or beef, rice, spices, tomato paste and onion); onions stuffed with meat and rice; and, for dessert, *halva* (a pasty sweet). Saudi drinks include raisin tea (made with water in which raisins have been soaked), lemonade, "Saudi champagne" (a non-alcoholic carbonated fruit drink), and Arab coffee flavored with cardamon.

A Western-style meal at a Saudi home would be very familiar to Americans. It might include lentil soup, a fish dish, steak, rice, salad and dessert. Fruit juice and Arab or instant coffee would be served.

SAUDI FEASTS

When feasts are held in the Kingdom today, the traditions of the desert remain popular. The main dish is still very likely to be mutton and rice.

This is prepared in the traditional way and is known in Arabic as *kabsa*. Whole sheep are stewed in giant pots or are roasted. When done, they are piled, in pieces, on huge serving platters and are surrounded by mounds of spiced rice. The platters are so big and heavy that two men are needed to carry them to the dozen guests (all men, the women eat separately), who sit crosslegged on the rugs of the dining room.

Juice from the meat mixes with melted butter on the rice to form a delicious if greasy combination. Side dishes of eggplant, eggs and cheese, round flat bread, and fruit or a sweet custard for dessert are also available. Since wine, beer or other alcoholic drinks are forbidden, fruit juices are offered instead.

Guests eat with the fingers of their right hand. When the meal is over, they rinse their fingers in bowls of water brought to them by servants. Tea and coffee end the feast. Shortly after the meal, guests take their leave. It is not the custom, as it is in the West, to linger and chat for a long time after dinner.

The Eid al-Fitr feast is a special event. When night falls on the last day of Ramadan, families break their month-long fast with a wonderful dinner which can last far into the night. Special foods include a traditional soup full of wheat, meat and vegetables; fried pastries stuffed with meat, pine nuts or cheese; a lemony salad; a lentil dish; yoghurt and chickpeas; and eggs fried with ground meat, onion and tomato.

A Saudi feast.

THE COFFEE AND TEA RITUAL

In Saudi Arabia coffee plays an important role as a social lubricant. To this extent, it takes the place that alcohol occupies in other countries. Coffee is served to guests as soon they arrive. Men meet at the local coffee shop to discuss the day's events. Feasts end immediately after coffee has been served. Because it stimulates people physically and socially, coffee has been used for a long time in the Arabian Peninsula. In fact, some believe that coffee originated here, near Mocha in Yemen, where fine coffee is still grown.

A brass coffeepot, coffee seeds and small cups for serving coffee stand on a table. Coffee drinking is a social institution in Saudi Arabia and preparing it is an art.

There is a special way to prepare coffee in Saudi Arabia. A small handful of green coffee beans are roasted over a fire. With a pestle, the beans are then pounded in a brass mortar and flavored with cardamom seeds. Water is then added. The coffee is brought to a boil three times, each time in a different brass pot, and is finally poured out by a servant in a long arching stream into tiny cups. The cups are filled only half way. The custom is never to accept more than three cups; holding out the cup to the server and tilting

A fast-food outlet in Jeddah serves pizza.

it from side to side is the sign that you have had enough and that the server should take away your empty cup.

Small cups of heavily sweetened tea are often offered to visitors as well. There is no special technique involved in brewing tea, but the same basic rule applies: drinking more than three cups is considered bad manners.

SHWARMA AND OTHER FAST FOODS

Shwarma is a delicious Middle Eastern fast food which is sold in the *souqs* and elsewhere in cities and towns in Saudi Arabia. It consists of slivers of roasted lamb carved from a spit, which is slowly rotated in front of a hot grill so that the meat is equally browned all over. Making a pocket of flat Arabic bread, the seller adds parsley, lemon juice, tomatoes and spices and presents the *shwarma* to you with a smile.

In addition to this traditional snack, Western fast food is also available. It is popular in Saudi Arabia for the same reasons it is elsewhere —it is quick, filling and cheap.

ETIQUETTE AND TABLE MANNERS

Genuine friendships based on mutual trust and appreciation are extremely important in Saudi Arabia. They open bureaucratic doors which would otherwise stay closed.

When a Saudi wants to entertain a foreign businessmen, he will often invite him for lunch at home. Members of the extended family, on the other hand, are frequently entertained at home in the evening.

A male guest will be introduced to a Saudi's sons and to his young daughters, but he will neither see nor meet the wife or any older daughters. It is considered improper for a man to inquire about another man's wife. Thus the innocent American question, "How's your wife?", would not be well-received in the Kingdom. Instead guests may appropriately ask how the sons or young daughters are.

Saudis do not call strangers by their first names until they know each other very well and have become friends. A Saudi man who is old and venerable, or a young man from a good family, may be accorded the honorary title of sheikh. If so, he will be addressed by it. An example: Sheikh Yamani. Otherwise, a man will be addressed as *Sayed* (Mr.). A married woman is referred to as *Sayedah* (Mrs.).

At meals there are three main taboos. Since the left hand is considered unclean, only the right hand may be used for eating or for passing food or drink.

The soles of the feet are also considered unclean; it is offensive to point them at another person. At a traditional meal where there are no chairs and guests must sit on the ground, they should squat or sit so the bottoms of their feet do not face another person.

And, finally, it is impolite to stare at other people while they are eating. Looking down at your own plate instead is considered good manners.

EATING (POLITELY) WITH YOUR FINGERS

Eating a greasy dish like mutton and rice with your fingers takes practice and, for one not used to it, is difficult to do gracefully. It is extremely important that you use only the fingers of your right hand.

The best, and in fact the only, technique for eating politely with your fingers is to make a small, compact ball of rice and small pieces of meat, using the fingers and thumb of the right hand. This little ball of rice and meat is then deftly popped into the mouth with the thumb.

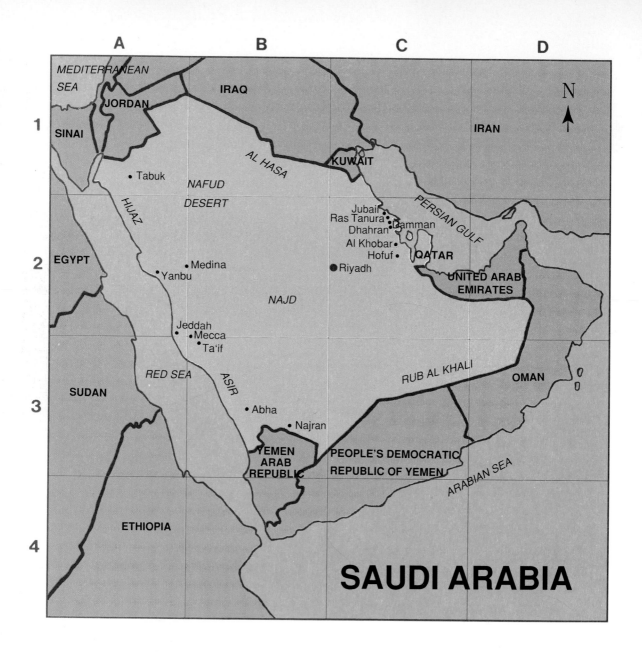

SAUDI ARABIA

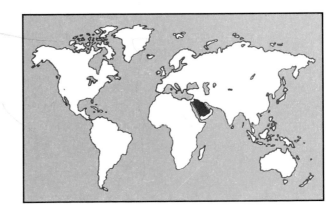

—— **International Boundary**
● **Capital**
● **City**

QUICK NOTES

LAND AREA
Approximately 865,000 square miles

POPULATION
An estimated 7.5 million Saudis plus an additional 3 to 4 million foreigners

CAPITAL
Riyadh

NATIONAL ANTHEM
Al-Salaam Al-Malaki Al-Saudi ("Royal Anthem of Saudi Arabia")

FLAG
Green with a sword centered horizontally at the base and the inscription in Arabic, "There is no god but God; Mohammed is the Messenger of God."

PROVINCES
Western, Central, Southern, South-Western, Eastern, Northern

IMPORTANT CITIES AND TOWNS
Jeddah, Mecca, Medina, the port-city complex of Dhahran/Dammam/Al Khobar, Jubail, Yanbu, Ta'if, Abha, Ha'il, Tabuk

NATIONAL LANGUAGE
Arabic

MAJOR RELIGION
Islam

CURRENCY
Saudi Riyal
(US$1 = 3.72 Saudi Riyal)

MAIN EXPORTS
Petroleum and petroleum products

IMPORTANT ANNIVERSARIES
Eid al-Fitr and Eid al-Adha (dates vary according to lunar calendar); National Day (September 23)

POLITICAL LEADERS
King Abdul Aziz (1876-1953)—the founder of the Kingdom of Saudi Arabia
King Fahd Ibn Abdul Aziz Al Saud—the present king
Crown Prince Abdullah—Commander of the National Guard
Prince Sultan—Minister of Defense and Aviation
Prince Naif—Minister of the Interior
Prince Salman—Governor of Riyadh

GLOSSARY

thobe   Long white robe worn by Saudi men.

gutra   The flowing head covering of the Saudi man, white, or red and white checked.

abaaya   Long black outer cloak worn by Saudi women.

Koran   The Holy Book of Islam.

hajj   The pilgrimage to Mecca, required of all Moslems who are able to go.

Ka'bah   The 50-foot-high cube-shaped monument in the Grand Mosque of Mecca, toward which Moslems pray.

sheikh   Tribal leader (literally, "elder").

souq   Traditional market.

BIBLIOGRAPHY

Lacey, Robert: *The Kingdom*, Fontana/Collins, London, 1982.

Lye, Keith: *Take a Trip to Saudi Arabia,* Franklin Watts, New York, 1984.

Mackey, Sandra: *The Saudis: Inside the Desert Kingdom,* Hodder and Stoughton, London, 1990.

McCarthy, Kevin: Saudi Arabia: *A Desert Kingdom*, Dillon Press, Minneapolis, 1986.

Schofield, Daniel (ed.): *The Kingdom of Saudi Arabia*, Stacey International, London and New Jersey, 1986.

INDEX